**If you woke up
tomorrow morning
and magically found
you had everything
you truly wanted...**

**How would your life
be different?**

To Barb –
May you find your
formula!

Wendy

Praise for
Shatter Your Speed Limits

"This fast-moving practical book is full of insights and wisdom you can use to break through any barrier and accomplish any success you desire."
- Brian Tracy
Author of *No Excuses (The Power of Self-Discipline)* and
How the Best Leaders Lead

"Wendy Lipton-Dibner has helped me shatter my own speed limits. She hired me for marketing advice, but soon I was asking her to coach me! Her advice helped me quickly double my sales, took my tennis game to a new level, and even improved my marriage. Her formula is simple but profoundly useful for anyone who feels stuck and wants to soar to new heights in any area of their life. Don't just read this book. Do what it says!"
- Steve Harrison, Co-Founder
***Radio-TV Interview Report (RTIR),* Million Dollar Authors**
Club and Quantum Leap Program for Authors and
Experts

"If you're stuck, if you've settled for a life that's not exactly what you want, *Shatter Your Speed Limits* is the tool you need to get on the fast track toward achieving your heart's desire.'
- Tom Hopkins
Author of *How to Master the Art of Selling*

"Move over Tom Peters and Ken Blanchard. You don't have to be a top executive to benefit from *Shatter Your Speed Limits*. All you have to be is human. Wendy Lipton-Dibner breaks business and life down to three simple concepts. Read 'em and reap the benefits of a self-fulfilling life."

- M. Constance B. Greeley, D.D.S.
Private Practice, Orthodontics
Past President Delaware State Dental Society

"As a physician, I see far too many patients whose illnesses are directly related to their lifestyles. Heart disease, diabetes and some cancers can often be avoided or cured with effective lifestyle changes and Wendy Lipton-Dibner's *Shatter Your Speed Limits* is a critical step in that direction. Her practical formula enables us to act on the impulse to risk the uncommon path and gives us the tools we need to succeed. If you are caught in the doldrums of consistency, paralyzed by the thought of imperfection or failure, or making yourself sick with an unhealthy lifestyle, *Shatter Your Speed Limits* will propel you forward and help you to achieve your goals. Life is too short to wait."

- Louis A Cannon, MD, FACC, FSCAI, FACP
Founder and Senior Managing Director BioStar Ventures
President, The Cardiac & Vascular Research Centre of
Northern Michigan

"Wendy Lipton-Dibner's *Shatter Your Speed Limits* reveals a springboard for action that will benefit any organization or individual. She has built a formula that helps us define the goals that really count and then reveals an attitude for achieving a real sense of urgency to make things happen. Her style tells the story in an easy-to-grasp approach that will hit home with the leaders of any organization, for-profit and not-for-profit."

- Don Pierce
Former President & CEO, Arby's Inc.

"Bookstore shelves are crowded with self-help, business development, and motivational books trying to accomplish what *Shatter Your Speed Limits* does. Wendy's book presents a common sense, accessible, and completely practical approach to discovering and finding a path to what's really important in our lives. Her conversational style effectively illustrates what everyone can do to overcome the internal doubt and ambivalence that stop us from achieving our most important goals. The book is filled with thought provoking examples that are helpful and easy to build on. It's impossible to read *Shatter Your Speed Limits* and not feel more capable, empowered, enthusiastic, and optimistic."

- Andrew Smith, MD
Vice President, Chief Medical Officer, St. Francis
Memorial Hospital

"Two ingredients found in far too short supply these days are passion and commitment. Wendy Lipton-Dibner brings a refreshing, needed blast of both in her exciting offering, *Shatter Your Speed Limits.* What's remarkable about this piece is that the lessons learned are told through an engaging story that includes personal epiphanies, paradigm shifts for personal growth, blowing through speed bumps that impede human progress and much more. Her enthusiasm for the story, the lessons told and learned and her love of people and their success is evident throughout. It's a 'must read' for anyone who seeks a fuller, more positive existence."

- Warner Lewis
Executive Vice-President - Director of Marketing, Peoples
Bank Host of Lewis at Large Radio

"Wendy Lipton-Dibner has done it again. Instead of talking AT us, she beckons us to follow an ensemble cast of engaging, believable characters along their intertwined journey and to share their 'Aha!' experiences along the way. As you begin to recognize parts of yourself in this quartet, you'll meet your personal internal 'Crew' who tell you—and each other—what to do 24/7. You'll come face-to-face with the carved-in-stone Rules you've been carrying around since childhood. And you'll see that anything you want to do requires Permission—your own to you. In a hurry? Speed-read this book in two hours. But to really benefit from the valuable insights in this modern parable—and savor its myth-busting ending—read it again, dig in for real and do the work. It's worth the effort."

- Bonnie D. Graham
Producer/host "Read My Lips" Talk Radio
(formerly "Up Close & Personal")

"Being a great storyteller, Wendy Lipton-Dibner leaves the reader with a visceral sense of the factors that can block personal success. This is one of the best books on personal growth of any kind I've read. Read this book to learn about the barriers you may have to success—and how to overcome them. What are you waiting for?"

- Nancy Collins
President and publisher, Greenbranch Publishing

"If you are a dreamer wanting to be a doer, feeling that you are at a crossroads in life, or if it seems you are just stuck in a rut, then *Shatter Your Speed Limits* is your solution. It reads fast and easy, yet is loaded with thought-provoking pearls that will help you to break through the barriers that keep you from reaching your goals. This insightful little book packs powerful and practical ideas that are easy to understand and even easier to implement. It will be the best $ you ever spend!"

- Daren Primack, MD, FACC
Pacific Heart and Vascular

"Wendy's masterful new book should be required reading for anyone who feels stuck in neutral but wants to live their dream. Her insights are profound in their clarity ad simplicity but make no mistake—this is a practical, focused roadmap with clear directions for navigating from a life of unrealized aspirations to one of inspired passion doing what you were meant to do. Wendy's empowering gift is a profound reminder of how short and precious life is, how fast it goes by and how to get on the fast track to make the most of it."

- Lonnie Hirsch
Co-Founder, Healthcare Success Strategies

"*Shatter Your Speed Limits* is truly a life-changing book! Wendy Lipton-Dibner speaks to the heart of everyone who realizes that time is money and that speed is a critical criterion for success. With her powerful Action Formula in hand, we have all that we need to break through barriers and move into high gear so we can achieve more in less time with maximum satisfaction. The dialogue in *Shatter Your Speed Limits* is brilliant and draws us into the story. We are more than observers—we participate in the characters' quests for success. Leaders of any size organization need to grab a copy and give it to every employee and then bring it home to their families. Bravo!"

- Mary Jane Mapes
Past-President National Speakers Association and author of *You CAN Teach a Pig to Sing: Create Great Relationships with Anybody, Even Impossible People*

"When people come to me wanting to 'get organized,' I know that usually there are deeper issues at play—issues of personal change that need to be solved to make things fall into place. *Shatter Your Speed Limits* addresses those issues and will enable my members and readers to get to the heart of the matter. Great questions for anyone to ask yourself about life and what's holding you back! I am excited to tell everyone how to shatter their speed limits so that the organizing advice we give can take root in the best possible way."

- Lorie Marrero, Professional Organizer, Author and Creator of ClutterDiet.com and National Spokesperson for Goodwill Industries International

Shatter Your Speed Limits™
is a trademark owned by the author and
Professional Impact, Inc.

The author's Web site:
http://www.ShatterYourSpeedLimits.com

FIRST EDITION

Cover Design: George Foster
Layout and art: Chase Rogers
Editor: Timothy W. Boden
Library of Congress Catalog Number: 2010910328
EAN-13: 978-1-4536-9170-0
ISBN-10: 1-4536-9170-7

IF YOU WOKE UP tomorrow morning and magically found you had everything you truly wanted...How would your life be different?

SHATTER YOUR SPEED LIMITS

FAST-TRACK Your SUCCESS and Get What You Truly Want in Business and in Life

WENDY LIPTON-DIBNER

This book is dedicated to my partner, my best friend and my husband, Hal Dibner, Ph.D.

Twenty-five years ago you walked into my life and blew away the clouds. Since then, I've had the profound joy of knowing the depth of your compassion, the breadth of your knowledge, the gentleness of your heart and the strength of your love.

Thank you for all of the richness you bring to my life and to the lives of our clients every single day.

You're my hero.

Contents

Prologue

It never ceases to amaze me how just a few simple things can change your business and your life forever. Even more extraordinary is the vast number of people who overlook the simple solutions in favor of the complex. How can we not? We're taught that the more complicated and difficult the journey, the more valuable will be the result.

So we work really hard at success. We look to gurus, read books, watch videos, listen to audios, attend seminars and pray to our gods. We try difficult systems, processes, programs and strategies in an ever increasing, desperate need to arrive at our chosen destinations. Forget about getting there quickly— we just pray to get there at all!

The truth is it doesn't have to be so hard. You can get what you truly want for your business and your life easier and faster than you ever imagined. All you need is a simple formula to get you started. The story you are about to read will give you that formula.

As a consultant and speaker, it has been my privilege to see individuals and organizations grab hold of the formula that is described in this book to make significant changes in their businesses and their lives. One woman used the formula to help her teenagers improve their grades, another used it to win a marathon and a third embraced the formula to lose 50 pounds and maintain her trim figure for 10 years (and counting!). I know a man who applied the formula to exponentially increase his sales, another who used it to build a successful franchise from the ground up and still another who used it to quit smoking and find his soul mate.

I watched the physicians and staff at a metropolitan hospital use the formula to improve the care they provide their patients while just across the river, leaders in a manufacturing plant applied the formula to align their team for increased productivity. I was honored to see one non-profit organization use the formula to motivate their volunteers to a higher level of performance while another used it to help challenged adults achieve greater independence.

There is simply no limit to what you can accomplish with the formula you're about to learn in this story. It's my profound hope that you'll enjoy reading this book, that you'll see yourself in between the lines of dialogue, that you'll act on the information you find here and that you'll let me know of your triumphs as you use this simple, powerful formula in your business and your life.

See you on the fast track!

Wendy

- 1 -

Say "NO" to Status Quo

David's heart jumped when the all-too-familiar vibration startled him out of his reverie. He slinked down in the chair, slipped his phone out of his pocket and held it well under the conference table so no one would see. Tilting the phone to catch the light, he squinted at the tiny words on his screen,

"Where's Ted?"

Quickly glancing around to make sure no one was looking his way, David slowly tapped one letter at a time, *"Dont knpw."* Texting was not his forte.

Just as he finished, the phone whirred again and a second message appeared: *"Could this mtg b any more boring?"*

David stifled a smile and replied, "Almost over. Corner Café after?"

"YES!" the screen screamed back.

"David?" a critical voice called out. "Are you with us or not?"

"Yes, Mimi. Sorry, I'm here," David replied, quickly stashing his phone back in his pocket. "My estimates are that we'll be able to raise $25,000 if we can get the mailing out by the end of this month. Otherwise, we'll miss the window before people leave for vacations, and we'll have to bring in volunteers to hit the phones in the fall. I'd like to avoid that if we can. I'll take the lead on getting the mailing out but I'm going to need some admin support."

"I'd be happy to help," Lisa said. "And what about Ted? He's got a huge team and he's always able to spare someone to..."

"Where *is* Ted anyway?" Chelsea interrupted. "I haven't heard from him since our last meeting, and I've sent him at least a dozen emails."

"The last I heard he was going to a pep rally or something," said David, "But that was nearly two months ago."

"Didn't he speak at the Dallas event?" Lisa offered.

"Yeah that was right around the same time," David responded.

"That's weird," Chelsea pondered for a moment, then offered, "I can come by on Thursday afternoon if that'll help."

"Thanks guys, that's great." David said.

"Ok," Mimi said raising her gavel, "then unless there's any more business, I move we close the meeting."

"Wait" Chelsea interjected, "can we talk about some new fund raisers for this year? I don't think I can handle another bowl-a-thon." David rolled his eyes in agreement and Chelsea had to turn away to keep from cracking a smile.

"I'm with you, Chelsea, we need some new ideas!" Lisa encouraged.

"How about a giant tag sale?" Mimi suggested.

Lisa closed her eyes and forced a smile. She liked Mimi and appreciated her many years of service, but her outdated ideas were impossibly frustrating. Lisa took a deep breath and started carefully, "Maybe we could try something different this year, Mimi. Perhaps something that would be an exciting experience that everyone would talk about all year! What do you think?" She underlined her question with a huge smile.

Mimi let out a big sigh and stared at Lisa with a look that clearly said, *don't mess with me.* "I think a tag sale would be lovely."

"We have to get out of this box, Mimi!" Lisa fussed.

Mimi turned her face away from Lisa's glare. "Zig Ziglar says *'if you keep on doing what you've always done, you'll keep on getting what you always got.'* If it's good enough for Zig, it's good enough for me!"

"Um, Mimi, that's not really how he meant it," David

explained. "Look at it this way: If we keep on doing what we've always done and all of the other non-profits start doing new and exciting things then they'll start drawing the attention of volunteers and getting more new donors to go to their events and there won't be as much left for us."

"That's nonsense. People give because they believe. End of story," Mimi dismissed. "Now I bet I could get my husband's quartet to perform at our tag sale. What do the rest of you think?" Her question was more like a dare.

The AACDA Board members eyed each other and one by one, they limply nodded their approval. The truth was, they didn't have a better plan. It was a tough economy and they were afraid to risk anything new.

"Wonderful!" said Mimi. "Now, will someone second my motion to close our meeting?"

"Second!" Chelsea cried out a little too enthusiastically. She'd had enough status quo for one evening.

A few people pushed back their chairs and gathered their belongings while some of the older members stayed seated, laughing over comments that were never meant for others' ears. A couple of people put away the folding chairs while others tossed empty Styrofoam coffee cups and half-eaten donuts into an overly stuffed trash bin.

David, Lisa and Chelsea were on their way out the door when they got sucked into a conversation by one of the newer Board members. Lisa excused herself and moved towards the exit. "I'll go get us our table!" she whispered sneaking away.

"Wait, we're right behind you." David whispered back but she was long gone. By the time he and Chelsea had finished their conversation, Lisa had already crossed the street and was entering the Corner Café.

"Hey Emma, how's it going?" Lisa said cheerfully to the

older woman behind the register.

"We're a little swamped tonight, but your usual table is open. Go on back and I'll get over as soon as I can," she promised.

"Thanks," Lisa smiled as she stopped to peak into the pastry case.

"She has no imagination." Chelsea complained as she entered the Café. "I'm not kidding, David, she is totally change-averse."

"I know it's bad, Chelsea, but no one else has stepped up to the plate," David shrugged.

Lisa perked up when she saw her friends. "Hey, you guys! What took you so long? We're at the usual table."

"Thanks, Lis," Chelsea grumbled following her back to the corner table.

David continued the conversation as he took his seat. "You know, Chelsea, Mimi's term is up next month. Why don't you run for Board Chair?"

"That's a great idea! You should definitely do it, Chels!" Lisa encouraged.

"Oh come on, you guys know me better than that. I'm not really the leader type. I'm more the point-out-what-the leaders-are-doing-wrong type," Chelsea laughed.

"I disagree," David challenged. "I actually think you'd be great. But in any case we've got to do something about this Board."

"Maybe we just need some new blood," Lisa offered.

"Good point. That would definitely help. At the very least we need a strong VP of Development," David said analytically.

"I'm with you, David," Chelsea agreed, "If I hear one more suggestion for a tag sale, bake sale, walk-a-thon or any other

-thon I'm going to scream!"

Lisa nodded, "You're right. We can't depend on soulful letters to help us hit our goals. There's much more competition for fund-raising than there used to be and we need to do something that will make people want to come to our events and support our efforts all year long."

"Hey folks, it's good to see you again," Emma interrupted. "Sorry it took me so long to get back here. What can I get for you?"

"Coffee, black," David smiled.

"I'll have a decaf, non-fat latte please," Chelsea said sweetly.

"Oh man, you guys are light-weights!" Lisa scolded. "I'll have a double mocha macchiato, heavy on the whipped cream and a chocolate chip cookie."

David and Chelsea locked eyes but didn't say a word.

"Where's Ted tonight?" Emma asked.

"We think he's out of town but we're not really sure," David shrugged.

"Oh. Well if you see him, tell him I said 'hi'." She turned toward the kitchen and added, "I'll get this right out to you."

"You know who would be absolutely perfect?" Lisa said.

"For what?" Chelsea asked.

"VP of Development," Lisa said with a *keep-up* tone.

"Who?" David asked.

"Ted!" Lisa said excitedly. "He's totally organized and he's got that take-charge thing going on, and on top of all of that he's got the kind of dedicated passion that only comes from having been through it."

"I know what you mean," Chelsea said. "I mean, we all want to do what we can to help, but I think it's different when you've actually lived it the way Ted did."

6

"Exactly!" Lisa said as she took a bite out of her enormous cookie. "None of us can even begin to understand what he and Ruth went through." She gingerly retrieved the cookie crumbs from her lap and neatly placed them in her mouth.

"I heard Ted speak about their experience once at an ACCDA benefit. He talked about how it affected both of his sons and explained how hard it was for him and particularly for Ruth. He inspired everyone to work harder and spread the message." Chelsea said.

"But where is he?" Lisa wondered. "He *never* misses our meetings!"

"Maybe he just got held up at the office. He's got a lot on his plate. On top of his work with ACCDA, don't forget he's CFO of Your Shipping Source, teaches nights at the community college and volunteers downtown every weekend!" Chelsea replied.

"Sometimes I think he just has to stay busy so that he won't think about what happened," David added.

"Maybe," Chelsea said thoughtfully. "I just think he's the kind of guy who can't stop doing for other people. I'll bet he's raised a million dollars all by himself this year - not to mention all of the speeches he's given to raise awareness."

"You know, we really should check on him," Lisa suggested.

"I'll call him tomorrow first thing," David promised.

Chelsea glanced at her watch. "It's still early. Why don't you call him now?"

"Good idea." Lisa added.

David picked his phone off the table and pushed in the digits for Ted's number.

"Why don't you use speed dial?" Lisa asked.

"I dunno," David sighed. "I keep meaning to program this thing, but..."

"The number you have reached has been disconnected. If you feel you have reached this recording in error..."

David looked at his phone to be sure he'd dialed the correct number and then looked up in confusion, "The number's been disconnected!"

"Huh?" Lisa asked. "Did you call his home number?"

"Yeah." David replied. "I'll try his cell."

Chelsea sat forward in anticipation as Lisa took another bite of her cookie.

"We're sorry. The cellular customer you are calling is not available."

"It says he's not available," David reported as he pressed the key to leave a message.

"So leave a message," Lisa coached.

David gave Lisa a *"what-do-you-think-I'm-doing?"* look and listened as the same robotic voice reported: *"We're sorry. The voice mailbox is full..."*

David looked at the phone as if it were an alien creature. "His mailbox is full."

"I'll text him," Chelsea said taking out her phone.

"Wait, something's not right," Lisa said. "His kids have school tomorrow and Ruth wouldn't let them all be out this late. Someone should have answered the home phone."

"Good point," Chelsea said. "Ok, *now* I'm officially worried."

"Maybe I'll drive by there on my way home tonight," David said as he checked his watch.

"Will there be anything else?" the server interrupted.

"Can I have a cookie to go please?" Lisa asked.

"I thought you were shooting for 20 pounds," Chelsea ᴠented.

ᵉ got a ton of papers to grade tonight," Lisa defended,

"I need the sugar to keep me awake!"

Chelsea caught the *leave-me-alone* look on Lisa's face and turned to David. "So, how's your book going, David?" she asked.

"It's not." David replied. I've got way too much on my plate these days. We've got a huge quota to reach by the end of this quarter and my boss is counting on my team to bring it home. Between my day job and the Board work... well, the book is pretty much parked in my desk drawer."

"But I thought you had it almost done." Lisa replied.

"Yeah, me too." David sighed. "But then I looked at it again and ...well, I don't know. I just don't think that's the way I want to do the story. I need a stronger title and the message isn't really right yet. Too many unanswered questions."

"I bet it's better than you think, David." Chelsea encouraged.

"Absolutely! Do you have an agent yet?" Lisa asked.

"Well, I met a few of them at that book-marketing seminar I went to and one of them gave me his card and told me to send him a proposal." David replied.

"Wow, David, that's awesome!" Lisa said. "So did you send it in?"

"Not yet." David said quietly. "I want to take this slow and easy and make sure I get it just right. Do you have any idea what goes into a proposal? The only thing they don't ask for is a urine sample—and I think that might be coming next."

"So isn't there someone you can call to help you figure out how to do the proposal?" Chelsea asked.

"They taught us that at the seminar but the truth is by the time I get home at night I just haven't got the energy to put into it," David sighed. *"Plus,* the agent wants to see my first three chapters with the proposal. It's gonna be a while before that gets done."

Chelsea picked up her coffee cup and looked at both of her friends over the rim. "How can two people who are so willing to help others be so totally lousy at helping yourselves?" she asked.

"What are you talking about?" Lisa said.

"I think she thinks we're failures," David grumbled.

Lisa suddenly felt defensive. "Why? Because I'm eating a lousy cookie? That's crazy. I just don't care about being thin like you do, Chelsea. I understand that it's important to you, but it's just not that important to me."

"Lisa, I love you and I don't care if you weigh a thousand pounds! I will *always* love you. The only reason I said anything was because you said you wanted to lose the weight. Just like David said he wanted to write his book. So all I'm saying is if you guys want something, then you should go after it! Life is too short to waste settling for anything less than what you really want," Chelsea's voice was escalating to the point of anger.

"Are you ok, Chels?" David asked carefully.

"I'm fine," Chelsea replied curtly.

"Ok, come on," Lisa cajoled. "You're not kidding anyone here. Whatever's going on you can tell us. I'd think by now we should all know our friendship goes way beyond AACDA. We should be able to talk about anything. I mean seriously—I've told you guys things I don't tell my own family. I don't mean to get all sappy here, but I think of you guys as my best friends."

"She's right, Chelsea. Talk to us," David encouraged.

Chelsea looked at her friends and sighed, "I'm sorry you guys. I'm just a little wired tonight. I've got my annual review tomorrow and I'm going to totally blow it."

"Are you kidding?!" Lisa exclaimed. "You are the best thing that ever happened to that company. I can't imagine them letting you go —*ever!"*

David looked at Chelsea and thought he saw a twitch. "Are you worried about getting laid off?"

"Yeah, maybe a little. People are talking about layoffs and, well, I overheard my boss say something about needing to do some reorganizing. That can't be good." Chelsea let out another deep sigh.

Lisa popped into overzealous cheerleader mode. "So what are you going to do in your review tomorrow—blow him away with those cool strategic plans you showed me?"

"I don't know. Maybe. . . But enough about me, how's the dating thing going?" Chelsea asked, desperate to change the subject.

"It's not." Lisa sighed.

"Have you had any dates at all?" David asked.

"Oh sure!" Lisa said.

"So?" he prodded.

Lisa looked at him square on. "David, no offense, but after what I've seen, the only men I'm interested in are Ben and Jerry."

Chelsea choked on her water. "Come on, Lis, it can't be that bad."

"Oh really? I went out to dinner with this guy and all he could talk about was his gym, his abs and his heart rate," Lisa lamented, taking another bite of her cookie.

Chelsea looked at Lisa sympathetically. "So you're not going to see him again?"

"Well of course I am. In this world, we have to be happy with the hand we're dealt and settle for whatever we can grab!" Lisa said with conviction. "I'm happy he wanted to date me at all."

"That's crazy, Lisa. You should keep on looking for the

perfect guy. You just have to keep at it," Chelsea encouraged.

"That's easy for you to say," whined Lisa. "You have the perfect marriage, the perfect family, the perfect body and the perfect life. What do you know about dating?"

Chelsea looked incredulous. "Perfect? Me? Oh wow, Lisa, you have a really weird picture of my life. Sure, my kids are wonderful, but they're far from perfect and I hardly ever get to see Carl because we're both working so hard to save up for the girls' college—not to mention braces and weddings and who knows what else. No Lisa, the grass isn't greener in my world. Far from it."

Lisa turned to David. "You'll notice she didn't dispute the perfect body part of it."

"Yep," David replied with a wink.

Chelsea self-consciously pulled her sweater closed. "Ok, look. All I'm saying is that you should go for what you want in life!"

"She's right, Lisa. Get the most out of life while you can!" David said. "Oh man, I sound like one of those infomercial guys. *'Order my DVD Success Series in the next 30 minutes and I'll throw in the bubble wrap—absolutely free!'*" he laughed.

Lisa picked up her drink. "Thanks, guys, but really I'm fine with what I've got." She vacuumed the last few drops from the bottom and then licked her straw. "Ah! Now that's what I'm talking about," she smiled.

The three friends paid the bill and walked out to the parking lot together huddling close against the cold wind. As they separated to get into their cars, Chelsea yelled into the wind, "Hey, let me know if you hear from Ted, ok? I'm kind of worried."

"Yeah, me too." Lisa called out.

"I'll keep you posted." David yelled back. "G'nite."

- 2 -

Do What's Right For You

When Lisa got home she went straight to her computer, clicked on her email and stared at the screen in total disbelief. "He's got to be kidding!" she screeched to the empty room. "I don't do that for *any* man! I have my limits!"

Lisa turned off the screen with a vengeance and sat shaking with anger. "I don't need this! In fact, I should break up with him right now," she added getting up from her desk. She strutted into the kitchen and threw open the refrigerator door so hard that the bottles clinked together. A jar tumbled out onto the floor and the glass shattered, catapulting sharp pieces in every direction. Leaving the door wide open, she grabbed a paper towel and bent over to clean up the squirmy globs of grape jelly and broken glass.

Suddenly the phone pierced the silence and she jumped, hitting her head on the kitchen counter and dropping the dirty paper towel and its contents back onto the floor.

"What?!" she yelled into the phone.

"Hey, it's me!" Chelsea said. "What's wrong?"

"Nothing," Lisa grumbled, rubbing the top of her head.

"Come on, Lisa. What's going on?" Chelsea asked gently.

"I dropped the jelly," Lisa mumbled.

"Huh?"

"Ok, be straight with me." Lisa demanded. "How bad do I look?"

"Oh, come on, Lisa. Seriously?"

"Yes, seriously, Chelsea. How bad is it? You can tell me." Lisa steeled herself for the answer.

Chelsea was determined to stay neutral. "Well...I think it doesn't matter what other people think. What do YOU think?"

"I think I'm fat and I frankly don't care. There, I said it. I just don't care. I'd much rather have the freedom to eat what I want when I want than have to sacrifice and be a slave to counting calories. And I definitely don't want to do the exercise thing. I mean, come on! Getting up early and sweating before breakfast? What kind of life is that?"

"Well, then you have your answer. What difference does it make what other people think?" Chelsea asked.

"Right," said Lisa. "Unless of course I hope to have half a chance of keeping this guy. He sent me an email asking me to meet him at the gym tomorrow at 4:30. That's *a.m.* in case you were wondering!"

"Lisa, if you have to change something about yourself that you don't want to change then he isn't the right man. End of story." Chelsea said. "Seriously, Lisa. It's your life and your body. Do what's right for you."

"Thanks, Chelsea." Lisa said, wiping the grape jelly off of her leg. "You're a good friend. Do you want to meet me for lunch tomorrow?"

"I can't. I've got that review, remember?" Chelsea said with a heavy sigh.

"Chelsea, now look. You are really smart and if you'd just tell them the ideas you've got, they'd be really impressed. Why don't you bring them in tomorrow and wow your boss? What have you got to lose?" Lisa urged.

"Yeah, okay," Chelsea said unconvincingly. "Hey it's getting late, so I better go. Are you going to be ok? Do you want me to bring you some ice cream on my way home?"

"You are the best friend in the whole world, Chels! I'm fine. Go home and get ready for your review. Text me when you're done. I'll be rooting for you."

"Thanks, Lisa. Bye."

"Bye." Lisa hung up the phone, went back to the fridge and pulled out a diet soda. "Ok, well, maybe I'll stop by the gym tomorrow morning—just to say 'hi.'" She took a sip of soda and grabbed the chocolate chip cookie from the bag on the counter. "Or better yet," she smiled, "I'll watch while *he* works out!"

- 3 -

Distinguish Threats From Opportunities

Chelsea drove to work the next morning thinking about her annual review. She got out of the elevator on the twelfth floor and entered the magnificent reception area. After seven years, she still felt awed by the grandness of the room with its mirrored walls, cathedral ceilings and bright lights. She smiled at the receptionists and walked quickly past them, picking up her messages in the little slot that had her name inscribed on a brass plate.

"I heard she's being let go," the blond receptionist whispered.

"You're kidding!" the brunette replied. "She's so nice!"

Chelsea entered her cubicle, sat down at her desk and picked up the photo of her family. Her daughters wore matching red outfits, Carl's tie was the same color as the girls' dresses and even the dog's collar was bright red. *"Lisa's right,"* she thought. *"They're perfect."*

She carefully replaced the photo frame and then opened her desk drawer and pulled out a file labeled *Ideas*. Leaning back in her chair, she opened the file and thumbed through the familiar contents. There were flow charts, spreadsheets, clipped articles and a few brochures with sticky arrows attached throughout. At the back of a file was a report entitled, *A New Era for Region 12*. She looked at her name typed at the bottom and brushed her fingers across it as if it were a piece of precious silk.

"Who am I kidding?" she thought critically, *"I could never pull this off."* She returned the file to the back of her drawer and turned on her computer just as the phone rang.

"Chelsea Browdy," she said cheerfully.

"Hi Chelsea," a voice said. "He's ready for you now."

Chelsea tried to sound more upbeat than she felt. "Ok, great! Thanks Sally,"

She picked up her pad and—almost as an afterthought—

grabbed the file. *"If I'm going to be fired, I'm going out with a bang,"* she thought as she walked back through the reception area, nodding again to the two women.

"You think this is it?" the blonde whispered behind her hand.

"I have no idea!" the brunette replied, "but I'd love to be a fly on that wall!"

"Me too," the blonde giggled, as she reached for the ringing phone.

Chelsea knocked on the heavy wooden door. "Come in Chelsea," Jeff boomed out. Chelsea walked in slowly and stopped in front of Jeff. He was nearly two heads taller than she, and just standing in front of him made her feel small and invisible. But it wasn't just his height—everything about Jeff was intimidating. His comments were like proclamations and his questions always felt like you were getting the third degree.

"Have a seat," he commanded. Chelsea slowly lowered herself into the huge, leather chair and waited for the ax to fall.

"Chelsea, I'll cut to the chase," Jeff barked. "I've been watching you for a long time. You're good—damned good, and I'd like to promote you to Regional Manager. But I need you to be straight with me and tell me if you think you can cut it. I plan to fast-track this company's success and in order to make that happen I need a fast-thinking, fast-moving, innovative leader. Are you a fast-thinking, fast-moving, innovative leader, Chelsea?"

"Absolutely," Chelsea said, raising her hand to give a thumbs-up. To her horror, her hand was shaking. She quickly dropped it into her lap and covered it with her other hand.

Jeff sat staring at her and didn't say a word.

"Well," she said, clearing her throat, "to be honest, I've never really thought of myself as a leader, Jeff." She silently prayed that she didn't sound as ridiculous as she felt.

"Well, maybe you should," said Jeff matter-of-factly. "I'll tell you what: I'll give you two weeks and then I want you to come in here with projections for increasing sales by 30% in Region 12 by the end of the year. You bring me an effective plan and I'll double your salary and give you an override on the entire region."

Chelsea stared at Jeff and reminded herself to blink. This would solve everything. Carl could give up his second job and the girls would be all set.

"But listen to me, Chelsea. If you blow this, I'm going to have to let you go. We're tightening our belts around here and I'm going to be shutting down your current position. So it's all or nothing—got it?" Jeff warned.

"I've got it, Jeff. Thanks for the opportunity," she finally said, trying to hide the quiver in her voice. "I'll get right on it."

Chelsea rose to leave and remembered to shake his hand. "Thanks, Jeff."

"Don't disappoint me Chelsea," Jeff yelled after her as she closed the door.

Chelsea walked slowly back past the reception desk clutching the file in her hand. Realizing she'd completely forgotten to mention her ideas to Jeff, she rationalized, *"Well, this'll give me time to tweak it a little."*

The two receptionists watched Chelsea as she passed by and tried to guess whether the news had been good or bad. It was impossible to tell from her face.

- 4 -

Dare To
Dream

Lisa sat at the Corner Café table and looked at Chelsea apologetically. "This week just flew by! I kept meaning to call you, but things were crazy busy at school."

"Don't worry about it. We're all busy," Chelsea smiled. "I can't believe we have two Board meetings in one month," she added. "How many meetings does it take to do a lousy tag sale?"

"Did David tell you why he wanted us to meet him here first?" Lisa asked.

Chelsea picked up her coffee and blew on it to cool it down. "No. I have no idea."

"Hey, how was your review?" Lisa suddenly remembered.

"It was okay I guess. My boss sucked all the air out of the room so there was nothing left for me and then he dangled Regional Manager in my face and gave me two weeks to prepare a presentation. If it's good, I get the job. If not, I'm fired."

"Chelsea, a promotion? That's awesome! Oh my gosh! That would be perfect for you!"

"I guess," Chelsea said into her coffee.

"Ok, I'll bite. Why do you sound like your puppy just died?" Lisa asked.

Chelsea slouched in her chair. "Oh, come on Lisa, you know me. I'm no manager. Besides, I have my family to think about. I can't take on added responsibilities now just when the girls are getting active in sports. I have to do the soccer mom thing."

"You don't give yourself nearly enough credit. Of course you can do this!" urged Lisa. "And as for the girls, I'm assuming this job would mean more money, right?"

"Yeah. A lot more money," Chelsea confided.

"So then wouldn't that mean that Carl could quit the other

job and be there for the girls?" Lisa nodded encouragingly.

"Hi you two! Thanks for meeting me early!" David said as he pulled up a chair. The server came to greet him and he smiled. "Hi, Emma. Can I have a coffee, black?"

"What was so important it couldn't wait until after the Board meeting?" asked Chelsea.

David dramatically swept a piece of paper out of his jacket and announced, "This!"

"What is it?" Lisa asked, straining to read it.

"It's an email from Ted!" David declared triumphantly.

"Oh, good! Where is he?" Chelsea prodded.

David looked at Chelsea and Lisa with a mysterious smile and handed them the paper. "Here—read it!" They put it between them and began reading:

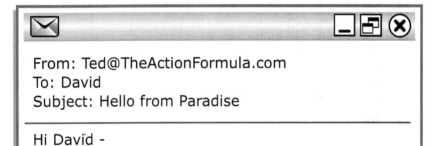

From: Ted@TheActionFormula.com
To: David
Subject: Hello from Paradise

Hi David -

I meant to call you before I left, but it got nuts with packing and the next thing I knew, I was here. It took a while to get everything set up and internet access is a little sketchy down here.

I don't know where to begin so let me give you the bottom line: I almost quit my job at Your Shipping Source. But then I figured out how to turn it all around for me and for the company and now I've got everything I want and life couldn't be better.

I'm opening up another division here and loving every minute of it. I rented out my house at home, pulled the kids out of school and here we are.

It's amazing down here, buddy. Everywhere you look, there are waterfalls and flowers. The locals are grateful that we're building another site here because we're going to bring a boom to their economy. Between that and the letters I'm getting from the home office, I'm feeling like a real hero right about now.

The boys like the school, even though they'll need to do some supplemental work over the internet with a tutor to keep up with U.S. grade requirements. Ruth is more peaceful now that we're all together. As for me, I got one helluva deal on a pre-owned yacht so we're living in high style. I figure if I have to be off the grid I might as well enjoy it!

You should see this boat. State-of-the-art, 80 foot, twin diesel, sleeps 8. She's even got a surround-sound theatre! I've named her The Action Formula. I'm the captain (of course) and Ruth and the boys are my crew. Ruth gets a little skittish at the higher speeds (this baby can sustain 45 knots) but she'll get used to cruising in the fast lane soon enough!

This is everything I've always wanted, and now I have it. I'm scheduled to move back home in six months, but who knows? Maybe I'll tell Jason I want to make this permanent!

Don't worry buddy. I haven't lost my mind and I haven't lost my edge. I know exactly what I'm doing. I just couldn't keep on going the way I was—driving the speed limit and getting nowhere.

Give my best to Lisa and Chelsea and tell them to stay in touch. I may be in paradise, but I never want to lose my old friends.

T.

P.S. I sent a check home to you today on the company plane. Do me a favor and bring it to the AACDA Board to disburse as they see fit. The cost of living down here is practically nothing and I can spare it.

"Wow," said Lisa.

David raised his water glass, "To Ted!"

"To Ted!" they all said and clinked their glasses.

They sat quietly for a bit, each lost in private thoughts. Chelsea was the first to break the silence. "What do you think he meant when he said he was driving the speed limit and getting nowhere?"

25

"Maybe he meant he got tired of playing by other people's rules. I'll tell you one thing: He broke every rule I live by. Every single one of them. Leaving his home? Taking the kids out of school? Living on a yacht? Come on!" Lisa said critically.

"Jealous?" David smiled.

"Of course not," Lisa replied. "But how can he just leave? He had a perfectly good life here."

"He sounds pretty happy to me," Chelsea remarked.

"That's just the honeymoon stage. He'll come back to reality and start craving traffic and the evening news in no time at all." Lisa said.

"I don't know, Lisa." David said. "He sounds pretty set."

"I just can't believe he really did this!" Lisa said. "The consummate, bottom-line CFO is gushing about sunsets and palm trees. I can't decide if I'm proud of him or mad at him or jealous of him!"

Chelsea laughed. "I know what you mean."

"So are you going to email him tonight?" Lisa asked.

"I already did." David replied.

"What'd you say?" Chelsea asked.

"Are you kidding? Whaddya *think* I said? I congratulated him and asked for his secret!" David said.

"His secret?" Lisa chimed in, "What do you mean?"

"Oh, Lisa, come on. Ted did what the rest of us only dream about. He figured out something he really wanted and he found a way to make it happen. An awful lot of beer has been consumed on this planet—all in the name of finding the secret to happiness and success. But he's actually *done* it. All I want to know is *how* he did it," David said, resting his chin in his hand.

"Are you ok, David?" Lisa asked.

David put on a smile. "Yeah, I'm fine, although, I am a bit curious about all of those rules you just mentioned. Why don't you tell us about your rules, Lisa?" he teased.

Lisa threw the rest of her muffin at David and they all laughed as they pushed back their chairs to go to the Board meeting. They walked out quietly, lost in the mental pictures they were painting of Ted—smiling on his yacht in the middle of nowhere.

- 5 -

When Experts Speak, Take Notes!

David opted to go straight home after the Board meeting. He'd had a long day and wanted to do some writing on his book. As he was driving through the empty streets, he looked down at his speedometer.

"Forty-four miles per hour," he announced into the darkness. He looked up and saw the sign on the side of the road that read *SPEED LIMIT 25.* He instinctively lifted his foot off the gas.

"That's fine for you, Ted," he thought, *"but I have responsibilities here."*

David walked into his house and kissed his wife hello. He grabbed a beer and said, "I'm going to go work on my book for a while."

Gillian shook her head as she watched her husband walk past her. He'd been working on his book for three years and was far from finishing it. What she'd read so far was pretty good, but he just couldn't seem to get it done. For that matter, he couldn't seem to get anything done. He was the consummate procrastinator, always starting projects but never finishing.

"What about the pantry shelves, David?" she called out hopefully.

"Oh yeah! I will definitely get to those this weekend," he promised. "I just have to get something done on the book tonight."

"You've been gone all week! Don't you want to spend some time with me?" she pleaded.

"Yes, of course I do," David sighed. "But I've got to work on the book."

Gillian turned away in frustration. There was just no point in saying anything else. They'd had this discussion one too many times and it never ended well. In the past two years they'd spent all kinds of money on seminars and success programs and he still hadn't completed that book—let alone finish cleaning out the garage. She put away the dishes, shutting the cabinets hard and hoping that he'd hear.

David sat down at his desk to write—but decided to check his email first. He took out his laptop and heard the familiar *Ding!* of his email. It was an email from Ted. He picked up his beer and settled back in his chair to read it:

From: Ted@TheActionFormula.com
To: David
Subject: re: The Action Formula??

Hey David!
Good to hear from you. Glad to know things are going well for you up there. Sounds like Lisa is off her game a bit though. Didn't her doctor tell her to get that weight off?

As for the name of my boat—it's funny you asked. I was just talking about that with one of my new friends tonight while we were sipping a Bordeaux and watching the sunset from the aft deck (sorry, couldn't resist).

I'll be glad to answer all your questions—but it's too much for email. Why don't you get with me tonight when you get in after the meeting. That'll be morning my time and I'll be able to take some time. Catch me on the Your Shipping Source chat site. The lines are fast enough there to have a decent conversation.

T.

David looked at his watch: 10:15 pm. *"Why not?"* he thought as he logged on and sent an invitation to chat. In no time the screen lit up and there was Ted. He was tanned and smiling, sitting in what seemed to be some kind of hut or— wait, was that a palm leaf fan spinning over his head? And what was that on his desk? *A mango?*

"Hey stranger! Good to see your face!" Ted beamed.

"Where the hell are you?!" David demanded.

"I can't actually tell you, David, I'm sorry buddy. It's all very hush-hush until the grand opening in two weeks." He leaned into the screen. "But I'll tell you this—it's like a danged Disney film down here!"

"What were you thinking going down there, Ted? This just doesn't make any sense!"

"I know David, but it does to me. I was up north juggling a Blackberry and an iPhone and carrying way too many keys in my pocket, and all I wanted was to get away from all that. Not a day went by that I didn't think about quitting and opening my own business, but I just couldn't make myself *do* it. Every day I'd end up at the same office."

"How come you never said anything to any of us? Did Ruth know about this?" David asked.

"Yeah, she knew. Actually, she thought I was depressed and tried to get me to read those self-help books. But you know me, David —I'm not a touchy-feely-soul-searchin' kind of guy. I'm a formula guy. If it goes into EXCEL, I'm *there.*"

David laughed appreciatively. "Yeah, I know! I can't believe I'm sitting here looking at you in a t-shirt with pineapples printed on it. And—are you wearing shorts? *Geez!* Who are you and what did you do with Ted?"

Ted grinned widely and winked as David took a more sober tone: "So go on, tell me what happened."

"Well, Ruth was really worried about me—I was pretty stressed out—so she came up with the idea of going to this motivation seminar. I don't know why I went. Those things have always turned me off. But Ruth has been really down in the mouth ever since, well, you know—and I thought maybe it would be good for her to go. So I bought a couple of tickets and we went to this weekend seminar thing.

"The place was packed with people. They did some stomp-your-feet, rah-rah stuff and got us all hooting and hollering about how great we are. It was good to see Ruth laughing again and I started to think maybe it was a good thing we went.

"On the second day, they got us thinking about our goals. They told us to write down what we wanted and why we wanted to achieve it. That was a no-brainer to me. I wanted to quit my job, be my own boss and live the high life. Oh—and I wanted a boat."

"Oh yeah—the boat. She sounds cool. Be sure and send me a picture!"

"I will—now shut up so I can tell you what happened! I do have to get *some* work done today!"

"You mean you actually *work* in that place?" David laughed.

"Of course. What do you think I'm doing down here?"

"That's exactly what I'm trying to find out! Ok, so go on—what happened at the seminar?"

"Well, after we had all our goals written down, they told us we needed to write out a plan for achieving them. They gave us their 'proprietary' forms, checklists, templates, online resources and on and on. I'm telling ya, buddy, if I spent all my time filling out their danged forms I'd never have gotten around to living my life!"

"I know exactly what you mean! I went to an author seminar

and they did the same thing. I came home with a suitcase full of books and DVDs and they keep sending me more stuff. I can't decide if I want to read what they gave me or write my book!"

"How's the book coming anyway?"

"Don't ask. So what happened next?"

"Ok—well Ruth had a good time at the seminar and she came back all pumped up. I guess I did, too. But the energy I got from the weekend drained right out of me as soon as I hit the rush hour traffic on Monday morning. I sat there on that highway and looked all around me into the windows of all those saps who were stuck there just like me. We were all driving cars that were less than what we really wanted so we could get to jobs that we hated, where we could spend the day bored to tears in meetings that went around in circles until we got back on the highway to sit in more traffic and head home to fall asleep in front of the TV. Who wouldn't be depressed?

"As I looked up the road, I saw a flashing sign that said:

CAUTION: SPEED LIMIT REDUCED AHEAD.

And there it was. My life summed up by a lousy sign. I was totally restricted by the speed limits of my life and now they wanted to reduce my speed even further and I was powerless to stop it. I just had to go along with the rest of the cars, taking caution and getting nowhere fast.

"By the time I inched my way to the office I was exhausted and lower than low. I decided to go to the seminar website, hoping it would give me some way out of this trap I was in. As soon as the page came up, I saw the head seminar guy in a video congratulating me on my decision to be a success. I quickly muted him. Then I clicked on a flashing link and found an article about how to write affirmations and use them to keep you positive. All along the sidebars were *believe-in-yourself* quotes and pump-you-up stories about how others had succeeded following their *simple* plan. I clicked another link and found an offer to buy their accountability software, designed to help me spend the rest of my living days planning out my life. I shut it off."

"Why?"

"Don't get me wrong, that stuff is great for some people. It just didn't do it for me. The seminar guy talked a lot about how it wasn't about the destination, it was all about the journey... well, that's fine for him but I had a destination and I wasn't getting there fast enough."

"I can't believe you were going through all of this and never told me. I thought we were friends."

"We are, David. But back then I didn't feel like I could talk about it. I thought I should keep my cards close to my chest, ya know?"

"I understand. So then what?"

"Remember when I went to Dallas to do that AACDA event a couple of months ago?"

"Yeah sure. Why?"

"Everything turned around for me on that trip. After the event I was on my way to DFW to catch my flight home when out of nowhere golf ball sized hail hammered my car. I couldn't see to drive and the noise was deafening. It was like getting caught in a barrel while hundreds of angry strangers are throwing rocks at you.

"I pulled into the rental car place just in time because the roads were getting so slick I could barely control the car. The ice just kept on coming down and by the time I got into the terminal, delays and cancellations were lighting up the boards. Man, there is nothing like a Texas storm to get your blood boiling. I got in line with all of the other wet cowboys and beaten execs and just kept watching as flight after flight got cancelled.

"The golf balls kept assaulting the glass behind me while some guy in front of me got into a fight with a TSA guy and got pulled out of line. By the time I got up to the desk, they'd cancelled my flight. Then while the agent was trying to find something else for me, the announcement came through that DFW was shutting down due to the ice storm."

"Ice storm?"

"Yeah. They get it pretty bad down there. All flights got cancelled and I didn't want to be stuck sleeping upright so I bolted across the street to the Hyatt to see if I could get a room."

"Oh yeah—I remember that place. My company did a sales meeting there. Nice place."

"Yeah it is. I lucked out and got a room for the night—but I didn't even bother to go up. I went straight to the bar and ordered what turned out to be the most important drink of my life."

"What do you mean?"

"I ordered the cheapest scotch they had. You know me— always watching the bottom line—but what they gave me was top of the line stuff. Unmistakable. Any schmuck would have known the difference."

"Not this schmuck. I'm a tap guy remember?"

"Well trust me, you can tell. Anyway the guy sitting next to me turns and says *'excuse me, I think you've got my drink'* and the next thing I know I'm talking to—well, I promised I'd never tell anyone his name, but let's just say he's someone you'd know if you saw him."

"You promised you'd never tell his name? Oh, come on!"

"Ok." Ted leaned in again and whispered, "Think casinos. And hotels. And skyscraping office buildings. And resorts. And... "

"That could be just about any billionaire on the planet."

"Precisely. And I'm not going to tell you this guy's name."

"Got it. So'd you give him back his scotch?"

"David, my boy, you're missing the point. Yes, I gave him his scotch. And then he bought me dinner and changed my life."

"Not too dramatic are we? Ok, how'd he change your life?"

"We went into Mister G's—have you ever eaten there?"

"Sounds snooty."

Ted smiled. "Yeah you could say that. It's a wood paneled library set up like a 1930's gentleman's club. Very Texas. Anyway, somewhere between the Wild Buffalo Carpaccio and the mesquite-grilled angus..."

"Wait—you ate wild buffalo? Ugh."

"It was good! Now stop interrupting or I'll never get to the important part."

"Sorry—go on!"

"Ok so at first I was like a teenager meeting his favorite rock star. Everything I knew went right out of my head and I had trouble remembering my own name let alone forming coherent sentences. But he was easy to talk to, and once we got talking, we just kept going."

"What'd you talk about?"

"Guy stuff—politics, sports, you know, but then we got into the kind of conversation that only happens when you're talking to a stranger you know you're never going to see again. I told him things I've never even told Ruth—about how I wanted to leave Your Shipping Source and open my own business and how I couldn't get past the terror of blowing it and not being able to support Ruth and the boys. He was great. Just listened and nodded and kept encouraging me to tell him more."

"Are you sure he wasn't some shrink pretending to be a business tycoon?"

Ted laughed. "No. If you saw his face you'd know him immediately."

"Aw come on, Ted, it's just us—tell me who he is!"

"I can't, buddy. You gotta understand—people are constantly coming at him assailing him for information, sucking him dry with interviews, hunting him down for sound bytes, all in the hopes that they'll get him to give up his secrets. The way he described the life it sounded pretty intense. I understand why he wants to maintain his privacy and I'm determined to respect that."

"That makes sense. Ok so tell me about the part where he changed your life!"

"He asked me questions—really interesting questions that no one had ever asked me before. He got me thinking about my life and my business and what I really wanted, and how I could make it happen. In no time he helped me narrow down what I thought was an insurmountable problem to three specific issues—I still have the napkin I wrote them down on—look."

Ted held up the napkin to the screen:

I want my own business
I have no idea how to do it
I can't get myself to quit my job

"That sort of sums it up neatly, huh?" David remarked.

"Right between the eyes. So then he asked me what was

missing. At first I didn't know what he meant but he kept on asking until I knew exactly what was missing: not enough desire to fuel my engine, not enough resources to carry it out and not enough permission to go after it."

"What do you mean by 'permission?'"

"I simply wasn't willing to change."

"Wow. No wonder you couldn't make it happen. Was it weird talking with this guy about all of this?"

"You'd think it would've been, but it wasn't. It was kind of like being in a movie that Ruth would watch—*stranded in an airport, the man sat alone in a bar and met the stranger who gave him a once-in-a-lifetime opportunity to change his life.* Only this was very real. I figured I might as well put it all out there."

"Good thinking. So then what happened?"

"I asked him to tell me his secret. He just leaned back into the leather chair, sipped his cognac and said *'you've got to shatter your speed limits!'*"

"Huh?"

"Yeah, that's exactly what I said."

"So what does it mean?"

Before Ted could answer a gorgeous woman scantily dressed walked into the room behind him. She smiled and in broken English said, "I so sorry sir...to bother...big truck here."

"Wow. Who's that?" David whispered loudly.

"She's my new assistant. We've hired a lot of locals to work on this project. They're good people. Not great with English, but they make themselves understood."

"Not bad on the eyes."

"You noticed."

"Didn't you?"

"I try not to. Ruth is finally getting used to the idea that people aren't much into clothes down here. I don't want to push my luck."

"Gotcha. So do you have to go?"

"No—I have a few more minutes." Ted turned and spoke to his assistant and then turned back. "I want to tell you about his formula."

"What formula?"

"The one he used to build his empire. He called it 'The Action Formula.'"

"Hey—isn't that the name of your boat?"

"Yep! If it weren't for that formula, I would never have been able to get this boat!"

"So what's the formula?"

"Basically, it says if you have this, this and that then you take action. The more effective our actions, the faster we reach our goals and the longer we can sustain and grow our success."

"I hope you didn't pay for that advice."

"David, the guy has clearly proven himself so do you want to poke holes in this or do you want me to tell you how he ended up juggling billions in assets?"

"Right. Go on."

"Ok, so he said that the difference between success and failure is all about three things: You have to want something deeply and passionately, you have to have everything you need so you're able to take effective action and you have to be willing to change. That's it, David. Three things. He drew it out for me. Here—I'll show you:"

Ted held another napkin to the screen:

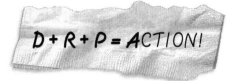

$$D + R + P = ACTION!$$

"DESIRE plus RESOURCES plus PERMISSION equals ACTION. He says it's the missing link between what we have and what we want in business and in life and that it is the one thing that got him where he is today."

"Wow."

"That's exactly what I said. Anyway, he explained that each of the three components have to add up in order to balance the equation. So, the harder the action, the greater our DESIRE, RESOURCES and PERMISSION have to be."

"That makes sense. But where does the shattering speed limits thing come in?"

Just then the woman reappeared. "Mister Ted...man say you come now!"

"Did you hear that, buddy?"

"Yeah I got it."

"Listen—stay in touch, okay?"

"Will do, Ted. You take care down there. And say hi to Ruth for me."

"I will. And try the Action Formula, David. It works."

"Hey email me those questions he asked you, ok?"

"Why don't you just call me later—that's tomorrow for you—and I'll talk you through them."

The screen went black and David pushed his laptop away. *"What kind of action do I need to take?"* he wondered.

Just then, Gillian popped her head in. "Are you working on your book or can you help me with the laundry?" she asked.

"Sure, I'll help you," David replied, closing his laptop for the night. "You're not going to believe what's going on with Ted!"

Gillian didn't answer.

"Hey—are you still mad at me? I'm going to do those shelves, I promise!"

DESIRE
+
RESOURCES
+
PERMISSION
=
ACTION!

ACTION

PERMISSION

RESOURCES

DESIRE

- 6 -

Discover
Your
Deepest
Desires

The next morning, Lisa and Chelsea went to David's office to help get the funds drive ready to go.

"Thanks for coming over to help me with this mailing," David said. "I thought you had a bunch of papers to grade, Lisa."

"Hey, I can work later. I'd rather help you get this done," Lisa said.

"Thanks," David said with a sigh.

"Are you okay, David?" she asked.

"Honestly, I can barely keep my eyes open," he confessed. "I spoke to Ted last night on iChat."

Lisa bounced around the room. "Cool! How'd he look? Did he tell you where he was? Did you see Ruth? How is she?"

"Tan, happy, relaxed. No he wouldn't tell me, no I didn't see Ruth but he said she's good. I'm telling you guys, I hardly recognized him. He was totally different," David explained.

"So what'd you guys talk about?" Chelsea asked.

"He told me about this formula that he used to turn his life around and I was up half the night thinking about it."

"What formula?" Lisa asked.

"He learned it from this mega tycoon he met at a Hyatt during a hail storm." David smiled.

"Oh come on, David. Next you're going to tell us the good witch of the north swooped in and sprinkled stardust on his head," Lisa teased.

"No, from what I can tell, that happened at the seminar he and Ruth went to," David played along.

"What seminar?" Chelsea asked. "I thought you said it was a 'pep rally' or something."

"I'm not really sure," David said. "He said that they pumped him up and Ruth had a good time, but that it didn't last."

"I went to one of those motivation things a couple of years

ago. I had a great time and it did give me a lot of things to think about. I thought it was really good," Lisa said. "I even bought a bunch of stuff afterwards, books and CDs. It was awesome!"

"Did you ever actually read the books or listen to the CDs?" Chelsea asked.

"Well, I started them," Lisa hedged. "But I got...you know... busy."

"Did it help you?" David asked.

"Well, it gave me some good quotes to teach the kids at school. I use them all the time," Lisa defended. "It gets everyone pumped up and positive."

"Yeah, I get that. I subscribe to one of those daily inbox things and I love those quotes. But the good feeling is over as soon as I read whatever is in the next email," Chelsea explained.

"Oh, I see what you mean," Lisa said. "No, the seminar didn't change anything for me. Not in any substantial way."

"Ted said the seminar didn't do it for him but he met some tycoon in a bar when he was stranded because of an ice storm, and the guy gave Ted his personal success formula. He sounded pretty jazzed about it," David reported.

"Like what kind of formula?" Chelsea asked.

"He called it 'The Action Formula.' It says that in order to get what you want, you have to take effective action," David explained, "and action only happens if you have the three components of his formula: You have to *want* something badly enough to make it happen, you have to have everything you need so you're *able* to make it happen and you have to be *willing* to take action and live with the consequences."

"Well, it's kind of a big 'DUH!' if you ask me," Chelsea said.

"I have to agree with Chelsea," Lisa added. "Sounds like he sipped a few, ya know?"

44

"Yeah, I know." David said. "That's what I was thinking too. But I keep thinking, *'This is TED we're talking about here.'*"

"I know what you mean," Chelsea said, "That man's a genius. In just two years he brought Your Shipping Source straight to the top of an industry that already had plenty of competition. He's a numbers guy—everything is about formulas and data and logical analysis."

Lisa started to giggle. "I'm sorry you guys, but I just keep picturing Ted at that seminar. Can you imagine the look on his face when some big linebacker-type tried to give him a support hug?"

"Oh I can totally see that," Chelsea chuckled. "And what about this rich tycoon swooping down to rescue him...in an ice storm no less!"

The two women tumbled around the floor laughing until tears were streaming down their faces.

David brought over another box of envelopes to be stuffed. "Ok, you two cynics. Let's just look at the data here: We're sitting in the middle of a crowded office, stuffing envelopes and looking out at gray skies and piles of dirty snow while Ted is speeding through blue waters on his own yacht, soaking up the sun and doing precisely what he wants to do surrounded by his family and totally supported by his boss. But, hey—I can certainly see why you're not interested in his stupid formula."

"Now just a minute, David," Lisa scolded. "We're stuffing envelopes because the volunteers pooped out on you and we're trying to raise money for a cause we all believe in. How is that a bad thing?"

A vein was throbbing on David's forehead. "It's not a bad thing. It's just that while we're busy helping all those people, no one is helping us. When's the last time either of you did something you really wanted to do or went after a goal that would improve your own life?"

Chelsea was astonished. "WOW! You're really buying into this nonsense! You sound like one of those motivation gurus!"

"Forget motivation, Chelsea." David said just a little too loudly. "I'm talking about real life here. When does it get to be *our* turn?"

"Well, I don't know about you guys, but I'm perfectly happy with my life." Chelsea clipped.

"Come on, Chels!" Lisa said. "Isn't there something you really, really want? What about that job?"

"What job?" David asked.

Chelsea shot a look at Lisa. "It was nothing."

"I don't think so!" Lisa said. "Chelsea is up for Regional Manager! That's a huge promotion and she's ignoring it."

"Ok, fine. I'm ignoring it. There's no way I could ever pull that off so why would I set myself up to fail like that?" Chelsea blurted out.

"I'm sorry, Chelsea," Lisa said. "I didn't mean to push."

Chelsea's eyes started to well up. "Don't be nice to me. I'm fine until people are nice to me" she said. She turned her head away so they wouldn't see her tears.

"Come on, Chelsea, talk to us," David said gently.

"Yeah, Chels, it's just us." Lisa added.

Chelsea just stared back at them. "There's nothing to tell," she said quietly. "I'm just gonna get fired and that'll be that."

"Ok, let's try something," David said. "Ted said we could call him if we had any questions about the formula. It's pretty late there, but I'll see if he's online."

"Great! I'd love to see him!" Lisa clapped excitedly.

"Keep stuffing envelopes!" David ordered. He walked over to his desk and logged into his chat function. As soon as he invited Ted the screen popped right up. This time it looked dark and there were little white lights in the background that looked like a Mardi Gras float. David realized it was the outline of Ted's boat.

"Hey you! Is it too late to call?" David asked.

"No not at all. No work tomorrow so Ruth and I went for a late swim. I'm just relaxing here. How are you doing? Is that Lisa in the background?"

"Hi Ted! Yes it's me! How are you?" Lisa yelled past David.

"I'm great Lisa! It's good to see you. Is Chelsea there too?"

"Hello Ted. I'm right here. David's been telling us some interesting stories about your adventures."

"I'm sure he has," Ted laughed.

"What are you guys on satellite or something? This is a killer connection."

"Yes—until we get all the lines from the plant to the dock, we're sticking with satellite here on the boat. So what's up?"

"I was just telling Chelsea and Lisa about your Action Formula and I was wondering if you'd be willing to walk us through it—unless it's too late?" David sounded like a teenager asking for the car keys and praying his dad will say yes.

"Sure, I'd be glad to. It's simple but don't let that throw you. This sucker is powerful. Ok—the formula is: **DESIRE + RESOURCES + PERMISSION = ACTION.** I'll start with DESIRE:

"DESIRE is all about wanting something. But I'm not just talking about "wouldn't-it-be-nice" kind of DESIRE. I'm talking about the I-have-to-have-this, I-want-it-so-badly-I-can-taste-it, I-have-a-burning-fire-in-my-belly and it's-all-I-can-think-about kind of DESIRE.

"Imagine you got your finger stuck in your car door..."

Lisa scrunched up her face.

"I know Lisa, just stay with me for a minute. If you got your finger jammed in the door, in that moment, you would be singular in purpose—the only thing that would be on your mind would be getting your finger free!"

"You got that right!" Lisa confirmed, shaking her hand to emphasize her point.

"Well, if you want to succeed at something that's out of reach, then you have to be that kind of focused, with laser vision aimed right at the bottom line reason you want it. All the gurus say that—but this is something a little different, so hang in with me.

"I talked about this boat for 20 years. But I wasn't doing anything about it. When I went to that motivation seminar they told us to think about what we wanted and why we wanted it. I knew why I wanted the boat. It was about status and fun. You know, the guy who has the biggest toys wins. And the thing with having my own business was a no-brainer. Who doesn't want to be his own boss? Clearly I wasn't doing anything to make it happen, but I didn't need a motivational seminar to tell me that.

"Then my new friend—did David tell you guys about my new friend?"

"Yes Ted, but he won't tell us his name. Who is this guy?" Chelsea asked.

"I promised I'd never tell anyone because he doesn't want people hounding him for help. I was just in the right place at the right time and he felt like talking. Sorry, ladies."

"Don't worry about it, Ted. Just keep going," Lisa urged.

"Ok, so when my new friend started asking me questions about my DESIRE, they were questions no one had ever asked me before. Then I realized what was different about them. At the seminar, they had asked me about first- and second-layer kind of stuff. Kind of like in sales seminars when they say you're supposed to find the *benefit* and then find the *super benefit*. But those benefits are obvious things that anyone would want. The secret is to figure out the deep down hidden reason we want something. That's what propels us forward.

"It's like when we watch TV commercials about hot new cars and while they're scrolling all the features of the car on the side of the screen, we don't even read that because we're too busy looking at the hot woman in the car. The message is clear: If you buy the car, you'll get hot women. And who doesn't want hot women?"

"I don't want a hot woman. Why should I buy the car?" Lisa asked.

"Don't interrupt, Lis. This is standard marketing stuff. Go on Ted," Chelsea urged.

"Well excuuuuuuuuse me!" Lisa huffed.

"Come on, you guys. Let him do his thing," David scolded.

"Don't worry about it. It's good to see all of you again. I've missed you," Ted smiled.

"We miss you too, buddy. So you were talking about the car commercials," David coached.

"Right. So I'd spent a lot of years watching those commercials and I'd never bought the hot car. It isn't like I couldn't have afforded it, and I actually did want it, so why didn't I take action and buy it? It's because the advertisers never got me motivated. They assumed that the hot women would do it for me but they didn't. Now, if they could have helped me figure out how that car would get me something that I *really* wanted in my life, then nothing could have stopped me from buying it. Obviously there were enough customers who were motivated by their ads and the dealerships sold plenty of cars. But I started to wonder: How many cars would they have sold if they'd mastered that one missing link to motivation?

"I became an avid viewer of commercials. All of them were sending messages about what their products would do for me, but none of them were addressing what I really wanted in *my* life. All their marketing research hadn't captured my personal DESIRES, and that meant they weren't capturing my business.

"I became excited, realizing that this was how my tycoon friend had built his empire. It was the missing link in marketing. I called a meeting with our marketing department and we reviewed our campaigns together. We were doing the same thing—creating images for our potential customers about what we thought the bottom line benefits were, instead of helping our prospective clients discover their unique, personal motivations for choosing us. We thought we knew what they wanted from all of our market research—but we'd never dug deep enough to really find out their hidden motivators. We had to find a way to make that happen.

"So I gave my VP of marketing the questions that my tycoon friend had asked me and the next campaign we hit a homer right out of the park. I never saw anything like that."

"So what are the questions, Ted?" Lisa prodded.

"Hey—this is my story. Let me tell it my way." Ted pouted.

"Oh, Teddy, it's okay. We understand that you're an anal CFO and you have to fill in every single detail. We'll just sit patiently and you go right ahead and take as long as you need honey," Chelsea sang in her best sing-song-mommy voice.

Ted laughed appreciatively. "Ok, ok, stop the sap. Let me just warn you guys—when my friend asked me these questions, it threw me. I wasn't expecting the answers I found and it hit me kind of hard. So just be prepared, because what you find out might not be what you expect."

"Sounds kind of ominous, Ted," David remarked.

"Well it is in a way. When I did this, I discovered that my deepest DESIRES had nothing to do with owning a boat or quitting my job or having my own business. It was what all those things would get for me. And I'm not just talking about the things you might think of like status or freedom or money. It was what *those* things would get for me—things that were far more personal and stemmed all the way back to a time long before you knew me."

"Really!" Chelsea said. "Like how far back?"

"Like all the way to grade school. When he asked me these questions, I unwrapped a dream I had long forgotten but it was still there the whole time. Someday I'll tell you about it, but the bottom line is once I saw the truth, I got a fire inside me the likes of which I've never felt in my entire life. I suddenly realized that I didn't really want my own business. I only needed to feel like I was *in charge* of my business and my life and that I was *making a difference.* That realization opened up my thinking and that's how I came up with the idea of opening the second plant down here. Selling it to Jason was the easy part. I simply asked him the DESIRE questions so he could figure out what was in it for him to let me do this thing. He gave me complete power and authority to make it happen, and we were off to the races."

Ted let out a big yawn. "I'll tell you what, guys. I'm pretty whipped. How about you grab a pen and I'll just give you the questions and you can work through them on your own time, is that okay?"

"No problem Ted, go right ahead," David said.

"Ok. Here you go:

"Question number one: *If you woke up tomorrow morning and magically found that you had everything you truly wanted, how would your life be different?*

"Get really specific here. Ask yourself questions like:

- What would I be doing differently, that I don't typically do now?
- What would I be looking at that I don't typically see now?
- What would I be hearing that I don't typically hear now?
- What would I be feeling that I don't typically feel now?
- What would I have that I don't have now?
- What could I stop doing that I have to do now?
- What could I start doing that I've never been able to do before?

"Question number two: *If your life were the way you've just described it, what would that get for you?"*

"Question number 3: What would *THAT* get for you?

"Write this down, David: After you've asked the first 3 questions, then keep asking yourself *What would that get for me?* Ask it over and over and each time it will lead you to a new answer. When you get to an answer that makes you laugh or cry, you've found your BURNING DESIRE. You'll know you're there because something will happen. Either your heart will skip a beat or start pounding in your chest or you'll burst out laughing or your eyes will burn with tears. It's different for everyone—but you'll know it when it happens. When it does, you'll know you've found it—*That's* the DESIRE that will rock your world. You'll feel like you've hit the powerband of

52

To find your DESIRES

Question #1:
If you woke up tomorrow morning and magically found that you had everything you truly wanted, how would your life be different?

Question #2:
If your life were the way you've just described it, what would that get for you?"

Question #3:
What would THAT get for you?

Keep repeating Question #3 until you burst into laughter or tears or feel a jolt charge through your body.

your engine and start riding through life at the optimal level of speed and energy for you."

"Wow, Ted, those are some pretty heavy questions," Chelsea said thoughtfully.

"You're not kidding," Lisa added.

"Just remember, guys, it's *not* that you have to want something important. It's that the thing you want has to be important to *you*.

"It's a lot like this boat. Everyone thinks it's cool that it has a maximum speed of 45 knots but what I finally realized is that it's not the speed that is so amazing. It's the efficiency and smoothness it has at the high speeds. And that's because it's got this really narrow powerband—that is, the range of operating speeds in which the engine most efficiently provides optimum power. So, the life metaphor goes like this: it's *not* how fast you go, it's how long you can sustain that speed without burning out.

"And that's why you need to know your BURNING DESIRE. It will sustain you through the roughest parts of the journey. Remember, the harder something is to achieve, the more you have to want it."

"So that's how you changed your life? You figured out why you wanted what you wanted, changed what you wanted and then got it? There's got to be more to it than that," Chelsea challenged.

"Of course, there is, Chels. DESIRES's only the first part of the formula. But you've got to have that before you can go on. Once you find your BURNING DESIRE, then you still need RESOURCES and PERMISSION or you won't succeed. I'll be glad to explain those to you another time but I've got to catch some sleep. Ok?"

"You're the best, Ted! Thanks!" Lisa waved.

"We love you, Ted, goodnight" Chelsea added.

"Thanks, buddy. I'll email you tomorrow," David promised.

"Goodnight guys. Now go find your DESIRES!" Ted challenged.

And with that he signed off.

"Cool!" Lisa exclaimed. "I know my DESIRE. I want to be thin without giving up any of the food that I like. Oh—and I never want to exercise!" she added with an evil smile.

"A valiant goal, Lisa!" Chelsea applauded. "Brava!"

"Thank you, thank you," Lisa bowed. "I do so love an audience!"

"Ok, Lisa, we'll start with you," David said.

"Ooops. Should've kept my mouth shut." Lisa said under her breath.

"That would solve the weight problem." Chelsea shot back.

"Very funny," Lisa said with a sideways glance. "Ok, Doctor Freud, analyze me."

"Ok," David said. "This is going to be interesting. So, if you woke up tomorrow morning and magically found that you were already thin, how would your life be different?"

"Well, I don't think my life would be different. I pretty much like my life." Lisa said.

"I thought you wanted to meet a guy," Chelsea said.

"Yeah, but that doesn't feel like it's a part of this to me. It's not like I would have the perfect boyfriend if I suddenly lost 20 pounds." Lisa said.

"Well, so why do you want to be thin?" David asked.

"I don't know," Lisa said. "I mean...I really don't. Sure, it would be nice, but clearly it's not important enough to me. I've gained and lost the same 20 pounds so many times. Then 20 became 25 and then 30 and the next thing I knew, voila!" she said, pointing to her hips. "Don't get me wrong, I'd love to lose weight, but it seems kind of stupid since I know I'm just going to put it right back on again, plus some."

"So it sounds like you'd need a pretty big reason to lose weight or else it just wouldn't be worth it to even try, right?" Chelsea asked.

"Right," Lisa confirmed. "I mean if you look at Ted's formula, the first thing it says is *'you have to really want something.'* Well, honestly, that sounds completely selfish to me. I mean, we should all be content with what we've got."

"Ted has more questions here. Do you want to try them?" David prodded.

"Sure but let me grab a donut first," Lisa giggled. "Just kidding. Go ahead."

"Ok," David said. "Here's the next question: If you woke up tomorrow morning and magically, without having to do anything to make it happen, you were thin, what could you do that you don't get to do now, or what could you *stop doing* that you have to do now?"

"Interesting questions," Chelsea commented.

"Yeah they are." Lisa agreed. "Ok, let me think. If I really were thin again..."

"Wait," Chelsea said suddenly. "What do you mean 'again?' When were you last thin?"

"Oh, a thousand years ago," Lisa said. "In fact, you probably would have thought I was *too* thin. But back then I was dancing 12 to 14 hours a day, so who had time to eat?"

"Wait! What?" David jumped. "Did you say 'dancing'? What kind of dancing?"

"Oh I thought I told you guys about that," Lisa said. She sat quietly for a moment, lost in her memories. Suddenly she sat up straight as an arrow, lifted her arms up in an arc and announced, "I used to be a professional dancer with the City

56

Ballet Company. I was damned good, if I do say so myself."

David and Chelsea stared at Lisa, totally dumbstruck.

"Why'd you stop?" Chelsea asked.

"I blew out my leg—right in the middle of a major performance. It was a very important night. There were visiting dignitaries from Russia. Even the President was there with his Secret Service guys.

"We were doing this Tchaikovsky piece filled with waves of big brass and pounding drums. Just before the end of Act I, with the music building to a feverish climax, I was supposed to twirl across the stage, take a running start and *leap* into my partner's arms right on cue with the cymbals! He would catch me and twirl me around and around and then put me down at the same precise moment that the next dancer jumped into his arms behind me. It was an awesome routine!

"The three of us had done this hundreds of times. I could do it in my sleep. Only on this particular night, as I came down and she went up, her foot caught my side and jarred me. It wasn't that big a deal but it threw my spin off just enough that I landed wrong and in one blinding second everything I knew ended.

"The pain was unbelievable and I honestly don't remember anything else except that I couldn't hear the audience. It was like they had stopped breathing and all I could hear was my heart pounding in my chest and a strange sound coming out of me that I didn't recognize as my own voice. And then that was it. No more music. No more audience. No more..." Lisa suddenly stopped talking and turned away.

A quiet tear dripped down Chelsea's cheek as she put her hand on Lisa's arm. David walked over and squatted down to be eyelevel with Lisa.

"No more *what?*" he asked.

"Me," Lisa replied with a strange little voice. She looked like she was no more than seven years old.

"Do you miss it?" David asked.

"Well what do you think?" Lisa snapped back. "Of course I miss it. Every single day."

"So, Lisa, if you got back to your dancing weight, would you go back to the stage?" David pressed.

"Can't. They had to put screws in my leg and no dance company would ever take a risk on me. Besides, I'm too old. Who would want me now?" She looked lost and miserable and Chelsea stopped trying to hide her own tears.

"I'm so sorry, Lis," Chelsea said softly. "I had no idea. And here I am whining about my family and my pathetic job. I have no right to complain. I'm so sorry."

"Forget it Chelsea. It was a long time ago. I'm way over it." Lisa was convincing no one.

"Could you teach?" David asked.

"Oh, great idea! I can definitely see you doing that, Lisa! You'd be a fabulous teacher!" Chelsea said.

"I already am a teacher," Lisa corrected. "In fact I've got 35 kids expecting me to grade their homework tonight."

"You know what I mean—A *dance* teacher. You could have your own studio!" Chelsea said excitedly.

"My own studio?" Lisa had closed the door on the world of dance and had never considered anything like this.

"Why not?" Chelsea continued, "You could *totally* do it!"

"Sure," added David, "I could even help you with a business plan."

"I don't know," Lisa said hesitantly.

"Ok, wait, we're not done with Ted's questions," David said. "Do you want to keep going? Maybe the formula will show us the answer."

"You guys are having way too much fun with this. Ok, sure, why not? We've come this far." Lisa said grudgingly.

"Ok here you go," David said. "If you woke up tomorrow morning and magically found that you were your perfect weight and operated a highly successful dance studio, how would your life be different?"

Lisa laughed out loud. "Are you kidding? It'd be totally different."

"So describe it to us. What would you be doing every day? What would you be feeling every day? Who would you be hanging out with every day?" Chelsea asked.

"Ok," Lisa said thoughtfully. "I'd keep teaching at the school because I really love those kids—but maybe I'd go part time and make room for some of the newer teachers that are looking for work."

"Keep going!" Chelsea urged. "What would your day look like?"

"I'd get up and go to the gym and work out because I'd have to be in shape if I'm going to work with those young dancers, right? While I was at the gym I'd probably meet a whole new bunch of friends—all male and gorgeous of course. Then I'd go to school for half a day and then to my studio in the late afternoon to work with my dance students into the evening. Oh! And I'd do a recital every year as a benefit for ACCDA!" she added joyfully.

"I love it!" Chelsea cheered.

David looked at his notes. "So if you did all that, what would you get to feel that you don't get to feel enough of now?"

Lisa sat perfectly still. She was facing David, but her gaze went way beyond him. "Happy...energetic...proud..." she stopped for a moment. And then, in a very strong voice she added. "I'd feel like ME again."

David and Chelsea didn't say a word. They seemed to know that they should just wait quietly.

Lisa broke the silence. "Ok, yes. It would be really cool," she began, "but this is why I hate this motivation stuff. It gets you all worked up and then there's no way you ever follow through. It's just a pipe dream."

"Maybe," David said, "or maybe not. How important it is to you to feel like YOU again?"

Lisa looked at David and then she looked over at Chelsea. She kept going back and forth between them, like a little dog waiting to see which hand the treat is in.

"How important is it, Lis?" Chelsea asked cautiously.

"It's everything," Lisa replied with a husky voice.

"Then how can you not do it?" asked David.

"At least think about it." Chelsea added.

"Ok," Lisa conceded. "I'll think about it."

"Good," David smiled.

"Ok, do me! Do me!" Chelsea said excitedly.

David and Lisa laughed. "Ok," David said picking up his notepad.

"No, wait! I don't need you to read me the questions. I can do it." Chelsea said bravely. "Ok—if I woke up tomorrow and magically found that I had the perfect life for me, I would get up each morning and take my girls to school, then I'd drive to work and walk into my brand new office with the title 'Regional Manager.'"

"What?" they said together.

"Ok, I know, I said I didn't want it. But I really do. I want it so badly I can taste it."

"Excellent!" Lisa screamed. "You should definitely go for it!"

"Maybe I will!" Chelsea said.

"What would that get for you, Chelsea?" David asked, reading Ted's questions.

"I'd meet more people, I could travel more, I'd make more money—lots more money!" Chelsea dreamed.

"And if you made lots more money, what would that get for you?" Lisa asked.

"I could save up for the girls' college funds and they could go anywhere they wanted!" Chelsea beamed.

"That sounds like it's really important to you," David said.

"You have NO idea," Chelsea replied.

"If the girls went to a good school, what would that get for *you,* Chelsea?" Lisa asked.

"I'd feel like I'd been a really good mom," Chelsea said.

"And what would *that* get for you?" David asked.

"It would get Carl's mother off my back once and for all!" Chelsea laughed.

"What about your own mom?" David asked. "What would she think?"

Chelsea suddenly stopped laughing and her eyes welled up. Lisa and David instinctively leaned in to lend support.

"Chels? What's up?" Lisa asked tenderly, passing the box of tissues.

Chelsea took one out of the box and held it to her eyes, but the thin sheet couldn't keep up with her enormous teardrops. She just dropped her hand and let the tears spill into her lap. In no time she had a big stain on her slacks.

"Chelsea?" David asked, "Do you want to tell us what's going on?"

She took a deep breath and said, "Ok, here's the thing. I never actually knew my mom. She died when I was a kid, and it was just me and my dad and my older sister. I don't know why I'm crying about this now. It's not like it's new or anything."

"Well, maybe there's something about this job that reminds you of your mom," Lisa suggested.

"No, I don't think that's it," Chelsea said.

"Is it something about your dad?" David asked.

Chelsea's eyes welled up again.

"I think you got it, David," Lisa said.

"I totally forgot this until just now," Chelsea said. "My dad always said that he felt guilty because he couldn't show my sister and me how to be good moms. Honestly, I don't know if I'd be teaching my daughters a good lesson by taking this job. I mean, what would I be showing them about being a mom if suddenly I'm coming home late and working nights and going away on trips?"

"I don't know what you'd be teaching them about being a mom, but I know what you'd be teaching them about being a woman," Lisa said.

"Huh?" Chelsea lifted her tissue and gracefully blew into it.

"Ok, look. If you get this job, you'll be showing the girls that a woman can do anything she wants to do if she sets her mind to it and goes for it. You'll be teaching them to go after what they want and to have confidence in their abilities. I think that's very cool," Lisa said.

"And with your work on the Board on top of all that, you'll be showing the girls that you can be successful and have a family and make a difference in the world all in the same week!" David added encouragingly.

"Now that's a message worth sending!" Lisa exclaimed. "I think you should do this, Chelsea!"

"Ok, darn it, I will!" Chelsea said clapping her hands gleefully. "This formula is really fun. So David, what about you?" Chelsea asked.

"I'm easy," David replied. "My DESIRE is to finish my book and be on the New York Times Best Seller list," David said matter-of-factly.

"Ok, so what would that get for you?" Lisa asked.

"Fame, fortune, recognition, power and influence...you know, the usual stuff," David said laughingly.

"No seriously, David. Come on, you made us do it," Chelsea urged.

"You tell 'im Chels! Ok, David, so if you had fame, fortune, power and influence, what would that get for you?" Lisa asked.

At that moment the phone on David's desk rang and he got up to answer it.

"Talk to me," he said comfortably.

Lisa looked at her watch and panicked. "I've got to get home or I'll never get these papers graded!" she said, picking up her purse.

"Hold on, I'll go with you," Chelsea said. "I've got to get home and make dinner."

The two women mouthed *Goodbye* to David and he waved back, listening disinterestedly to the voice on the other end of the phone and wondering, *"So what is my DESIRE?"*

REMEMBER:

It's not that you have to want something important. It's that the thing you want has to be important to you.

It's not how fast you go, it's how long you can sustain that speed without burning out.

The harder something is to achieve, the more you have to want it.

- 7 -

Gather
Your
Resources

The next morning, David sat down for his coffee and smiled as Gillian brought him some eggs.

He looked up at her with guilty eyes. "What did I do to end up with someone wonderful like you?"

"It's ok, I'm not mad at you any more," Gillian smiled. She put her hand on his shoulder and struck a Scarlet O'Hara pose. "How could I stay mad at you? You are just the sweetest, most loving, most giving man in the whole, wide world," she cooed and kissed the tip of his nose.

"Ok, Gil, enough," he said laughing, "I'll help you get the snow off your car."

"Now, David, come on, I meant every word," she purred.

"Yes, dear, I know. Go ahead and start it up so the defroster gets going, and I'll be right out," he instructed. "I just want to check my email before I head out."

Gillian threw on her coat and fairly skipped out the door while David took out his phone. The first email was from Ted.

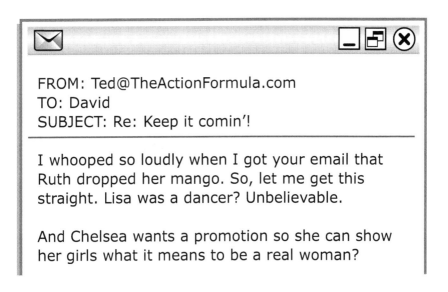

FROM: Ted@TheActionFormula.com
TO: David
SUBJECT: Re: Keep it comin'!

I whooped so loudly when I got your email that Ruth dropped her mango. So, let me get this straight. Lisa was a dancer? Unbelievable.

And Chelsea wants a promotion so she can show her girls what it means to be a real woman?

I don't know about you, Buddy, but that's not my definition of a "real woman." On the other hand, I told Ruth and she totally got it, so it's probably a guy/gal thing.

Anyway, if you want to do the RESOURCES part of the formula, give me a call later.

T.

David helped Gillian with her car and then bounded up the stairs to see if he could catch Ted before it was too late. He clicked on the buddy list and Ted popped onto his screen.

"Hey—did I catch you at a bad time?" David asked.

"Nope—just winding down after a nice dinner. You should see Ruth clean a fish. It's a vision and a half."

"Ruth is cleaning fish? What are you *doing* down there?"

"The boys caught the fish and the natives taught her how to clean and cook it. Better than anything I ever had stateside."

"I bet. So listen, I've got to get to work—can you just tell me about the RESOURCES thing?"

"I'm starting to feel like Yoda. Ok. **RESOURCES are all the things, skills and people you need to be able to get what you want.**

"I used to think of RESOURCES as the things we need to get a job done—you know—employees, time, money, skills, supplies, etc. But I already had all those things and they weren't getting me what I wanted.

"Remember, I told you that when I answered my friend's DESIRE questions, I discovered that what I really wanted was to be *in charge* and to *make a difference?*"

"Yes. You said that was the real reason you wanted to have your own business."

"Right. So, my next step was to figure out how to make it happen. But it was hard to wrap my head around how I would start my own business. I was drowning in questions like, *Where would I get my clients? How was I going to learn all the things I didn't know? Where would I get the seed money?* And on and on.

"My Dallas guy said that many people fall short of their goals because they spend too much time doing what I was doing—focusing on questions that lead them to be overwhelmed by everything they don't know, don't have, can't do, etc."

"Well, duh! How else are you supposed to think about goals—especially ones that require so many changes like the one you were looking at?"

"He encouraged me to stop thinking about what I didn't have or know and focus first on what I already have. He asked me questions about my existing skills, contacts and assets, and I could actually feel my brain twisting inside my skull."

"What do you mean?"

"I saw my situation from an entirely different perspective. When I thought about what skills I bring to the table and the people I knew who could help me I suddenly felt a sense of power I hadn't felt before. Instead of focusing on how impossible it all seemed, suddenly everything seemed totally feasible. I started thinking about my abundance of riches and how I could use those to my advantage and then realized that I absolutely *could* open my own business. So then the question became, *Would that be the best solution to help me reach my DESIRES?*

"We talked about it some more and I realized that the fastest route to get me to feel in charge and make a real difference would be to use the Your Shipping Source infrastructure to create a new business in a developing country. I never would have thought of that if we hadn't gone through this logic stream."

"Brilliant."

"Thanks—I kinda thought so too!"

"So how did you figure out what RESOURCES you'd need for that?"

"Once I figured out the RESOURCES that I already had, the next step was to figure out what was *missing* from my current RESOURCES and particularly *who* was missing that could help me take action and get what I wanted."

"It makes a lot of sense. So walk me through this now. How did you do it?"

"Just go through the questions my guy asked me."

"What questions?"

"Ok—got your pen?"

"Yep."

"Once you know your BURNING DESIRE, then ask yourself these questions:

1. **What skills, assets and contacts have you already got that would help you get what you want?**
2. **What's missing from your current set of RESOURCES that keeps you from being able to get what you want?**
3. **How will you get each thing?**
4. **Who will you get to help you?**
5. **What's your deadline for having it in place?**

"The people factor was probably the biggest roadblock for me—that's question number four. To be honest, I'd never been the kind of guy who would ask for help or coaching or

To Find Your
RESOURCES

Question #1:
What skills, assets and contacts have you already got that would help you get what you want?

Question #2:
What's missing from you current set of RESOURCES that keeps you from being able to get what you want?

Question #3:
How will you get each thing?

Question #4:
Who will you get to help you?

Question #5:
What's your deadline for having it in place?

anything that would let anyone know that I didn't really know what I was doing."

"No one likes admitting that. Except maybe in sports. Somehow it's okay to get coached on the field. Just not in business or personal stuff. I have a friend who hates asking for help. He won't even go to the doctor when he gets sick."

"I wasn't much different. But now I see how stupid that was. How are we supposed to build success if we don't know what we should be doing? Hell, I didn't even know what questions to ask let alone who to ask."

"Been there buddy."

"Ok, so the point is that you need to ask for help. The bigger your DESIRE, the more you need effective help to make it happen. In fact, the best way to make it happen is to work the Action Formula with other people. I discovered the hard way that *doing it alone keeps you alone.*"

"You're right. It's just that sometimes it seems easier to do it alone than to have to deal with people."

"I know. I've been there believe me. But I gotta tell ya— my Dallas dude set me straight. He said, '*Ted, if you could've done this alone you would have pulled it off a long time ago*' and he was right. He coached me through this thing and I never could have done it as fast without him."

"I can't believe you lucked out and found that guy."

"Yeah I know. And now you've got me, and you're already passing it on to Chelsea and Lisa—and they will pass it on to other people. That's the way it works: **Success is greatest when everyone works the Action Formula together.**"

"Ok, so can you give me an example of how to do the RESOURCE questions?"

"Tell you what. When we get off of this call I'll email you

a part of the RESOURCE list I created that night in Dallas. He just talked me through it and I wrote it out on a series of napkins. I ultimately put it into Excel, but do whatever works for you. I'm not gonna send the whole thing because it will bore you, but it will give you a good idea of what I'm talking about. It doesn't have to be perfect, David. Just get it down on paper because it will help you think it through so you can see a logical progression."

"Ok thanks, I'll look forward to seeing it."

"Ok—gotta run. Ruth's got this Yoga video she wants me to do with her tonight. Yeah, I know. Namaste and all that crap. But health is part of my new RESOURCE plan, so I'm committed to this."

David started to snicker.

"Stop laughing! I'll catch you later."

David closed the chat screen and went to finish getting dressed. As he was knotting his tie, he heard a *Ding!* from his laptop. It was an email from Ted with the list he'd promised. David double-clicked on the paperclip icon and opened the file.

"Ever the CFO," David laughed to himself, as he looked at the highly organized chart Ted had created.

MY RESOURCES

What have I already got that I can use to help me get what I want?

SKILLS:
20 yrs finance and operations, Executive leadership, BOD, speaking, strategic planning, project management

PEOPLE:
Ruth, Jason, Craig, Laurie, Kelly

ASSETS:
Savings account, electronics, records, contacts

What's Missing That I'll Need	How I'll Get It	Who I'll Get To Help Me	Deadline for Getting It
A project of my own under the Your Shipping Source umbrella	Open a site far enough away that I will be independent in an area that will cut our international routes in half	Jason needs to okay this, then take it to the BOD	September 1
The perfect location	Research	Doug	October 1
Specs	Build task force	Geoffrey, Steve, Brenda	November 1
On site staffing	Recruit and build	Barbara in HR and university counselors for internship students	November 1
Rent the house	Realtor	Amanda	December 1
A boat we can live and play on	1. Search online for auctions 2. Talk to brokers 3. Down payment	Ruth	November 1
Dock	Research options	1. Gordie 2. Local realtor	November 1
School for the boys	Ruth	Ruth	November 1
Health	1. Exercise daily 2. Eat low-carb 3. Limit my beer 4. Play with the boys	1. Craig 2. Ruth 3. Ruth 4. Mark & Kevin	Today and every day

David printed out the attachment and left for work. By the time he thought about it again, the day was over and it was time to leave for the ACCDA Volunteers' meeting.

As he was driving to the meeting, he thought about Ted's questions. *"What's missing that's keeping me from getting this book done and on the Times Best Seller list?"* he wondered. He turned onto the highway and thought as he drove.

"I have everything I need." David said to the passing cars. "I have my outline, I'm a good writer, I have plenty of time on the weekends and at night, I've got all the books and information on how to get publicity and market the book from the seminar and I've got the literary agent who said he was interested. No, wait. I'm supposed to ask 'what's *missing.*'

"Ok, the only thing missing is a publisher, but that's not going to happen without a book. And the book's not going to happen until I really understand what I want to write about. That's what's missing! I still haven't figured out the real message of the book and I can't do that until I figure out why I'm writing the damned thing.

"Yes! That's what's missing—I still haven't figured out my DESIRE! I'm going to have to go through those initial questions one of these days."

Frustrated, he turned on the radio to his favorite talk show.

"So, what made you decide to write your book?" the velvety voice asked.

David burst out laughing and leaned over to turn up the volume just as his cell phone started to ring. Instead, he turned down the sound and answered his phone.

"Talk to me," he said mechanically.

"David, it's Lisa. I can't make the meeting. Can you tell them I'm sorry?" she asked.

"Sure, Lisa. Is everything all right?" he asked.

"Yeah, I'm fine. I've just got a lot on my plate and the parent-teacher conferences are tomorrow and I still have to get my room ready and it's a mess," she said frantically.

"Ok, don't worry. You just do what you need to do. I'll cover for you," he promised.

"You're my hero! I owe you!" Lisa called out as she was hanging up.

David heard the line click off. "You're very welcome!" he said to no one.

He reached over and turned the radio back up.

This is Sky Radar Joe and I'm sorry to tell you, folks, that if you have somewhere you need to be or want to be, you're not going to make it any time soon. This traffic is going nowhere fast. In fact, if it were going any slower these people would be going backwards...

"Perfect," he said sarcastically.

The volunteers' meeting ran late and when it was over, David and Chelsea catapulted across the street to get a hit of java at the Corner Café.

Chelsea took a huge swallow and fanned her mouth to cool it down while she looked over the chart David had laid out on the table. "He always was a stickler for details," said Chelsea as she looked at Ted's email.

"Yeah, I always appreciated that about him," David said. "That's never been my thing. I'd rather leave that to the Ted's of the world."

"Not me. I love this stuff. I'm actually a major planner. I make lists to remind myself to make lists. The more I have things detailed out, the better I feel," said Chelsea.

"Well, here, I'll be your secretary," said David as he pulled a pen out of his breast pocket. "Tell me—what RESOURCES do you already have that will help you do the Regional Manager's job?"

"Well, I have an MBA with 10 years in sales and marketing, I know Region 12 really well, I have a lot of contacts in the area, I am a good idea-person but I am also very organized and I always finish what I start," Chelsea said.

"Good. What people are in your life that you would consider as RESOURCES?" David asked.

"Well, of course you and Lisa, Carl, and there are some people at work you don't know."

"Ok good. Now what about assets? What have you got that you bring to the table apart from your skills?"

"You mean like computers and stuff?"

"Right."

"Everything I have belongs to the company. Except my contacts... and my idea for maximizing our position in the region. That's all mine," she said proudly.

"Ok, great! Now tell me—what are the missing RESOURCES you need so you'll be able to take on the Regional Manager's job?"

"Cool!" Chelsea chirped. This sounded like fun.

"First," she began, "I really don't understand my boss' vision for the whole thing. He said he wants to increase sales by 30% but where does he see all of this going long term? How much freedom do I have to design my strategies? What's my budget? Can I build a new team, or are we stuck with who we've got? Are we looking to expand beyond the geographical boundaries of the current mapping? What can we eliminate in our line to make room for new product, and are we ready to launch a new line? Who can I get cozy with in the Marketing Department so that I can get some help with my internal marketing plan, and...."

"Ok, great start!" David said encouragingly. "It sounds like you've got it all in your head and we just need to get it organized for you. So, the first thing I wrote on your RESOURCE list is the *boss' vision*. Now, how will you get it?"

"At our meeting on Monday—Oh! I guess it would help if I actually tell him I want the job!" she laughed. "You know, I'm supposed to do a presentation for him to actually win the position but that's no biggie. I've had that presentation sitting in my drawer for three months. It's really good—I just never thought I would actually be showing it to anyone, and... Wait a minute! Am I really gonna *do* this thing?" She suddenly looked terrified.

"You're not committed to anything yet. We're just making a list here. And what are your options really—you either go for the promotion or take the hit and grab your pink slip," David reminded her.

"Right," said Chelsea.

"Now, who will you get to help you prepare for the meeting?" David asked.

Chelsea smiled her cutest smile, cocked her head, batted her eyelashes, and fanned herself with her hand.

"You've been taking lessons from my wife," David said smiling. "Yes, Chelsea, I'd be happy to help you."

Chelsea beamed back a grateful smile.

"Ok, we know the deadline—that's Monday," David said, as he filled in the spaces on the chart.

The two friends worked on until all of the customers were

gone and the servers were counting the register.

"Do you need us to leave?" David called over to the workers respectfully.

"No you're fine," one young woman replied. "We've still got a lot of cleanup to do. Stay as long as you like."

Within an hour they had completed the rest of Chelsea's Resource list:

MY RESOURCES

What Have I Already Got?

Skills: MBA, 10 yrs sales/mktg
Region 12 savvy, Good idea person
Very organized, Always start
what I finish

People:
Carl, David, Lisa
People at work

Assets:
Lots of contacts
Strategic Plan for
Region 12

What's Missing That I'll Need	How I'll Get It	Who I'll Get To Help Me	Deadline for Getting It
A killer presentation	Done but needs to be fine-tuned and practiced	David	Sunday
The boss' vision	Create 3 specific questions	David	Sunday
3 Mentors - Other Regional Managers	Request phone interviews Create a list of questions	Jack Brian Tom	2 weeks after accepting the position offer
Extra coverage for the girls in case I have to work overtime or travel	1. Talk with Carl 2. Talk with the girls' coaches about after-school activities 3. Give heads up to Rachel about covering carpools 4. Talk to Carl's Mom (only as a last resort)	Lisa	Tomorrow
Health	1. Make appt to see Dr. Stein just in case 2. Drink more water 3. Change workout to am	1. Me 2. Me 3. Karen	Today
Cheerleaders	Ask for support	Carl, Lisa and David	Today

As Chelsea sat wondering what else was missing, her cell phone started vibrating in her bag. She fished it out from the very bottom with experienced precision.

"Mom, you have to come home NOW!" the voice exclaimed.

"It's Brooke," Chelsea whispered to David. "What's wrong, honey?"

"Mom, I'm not kidding, you have to come home NOW!" her nine-year-old repeated. She could barely catch her breath.

"What's happening, Brooke?" Chelsea asked calmly. It certainly wasn't the first time one of her girls had called sounding panicked, but it was always about a missing hairbrush, a broken CD or a major dispute over whose turn it was to walk the dog. She'd long ago learned not to react until she got all the data.

"Mom, I have to wash my hair right now and Dori won't come out of the bathroom!" Brooke explained dramatically.

Chelsea covered the phone and whispered to David, "It's ok. Girl stuff." She moved the phone back to her ear and asked, "Ok, Brookie, what have you thought to do about this?"

"ME? I'm only a kid. You're the mom. It's your job to fix it!" Brooked whined.

Chelsea stifled a laugh and put on her serious mom voice. "Ok, honey, let's figure this out. What can you imagine that would allow Dori to finish what she's doing in the bathroom and also let you get your hair washed before you go to bed?" Chelsea probed.

"Well, I guess I could wash my hair in *your* bathroom." Brooke said manipulatively, knowing full well that Chelsea's bathroom was her private domain.

"Nice try honey. Can you think of anything else?" Chelsea asked hopefully.

"Well, maybe I could tell Dori that I'll walk the dog for her if she hurries up and comes out now?" Brooke asked cautiously.

80

"Now *that's* using your head, Brooke! Good for you!" Chelsea said proudly.

"Or else maybe I could tell her she can listen to my CDs," Brooke added.

"I think that would be really lovely. Good for you, Brooke. Now you better hurry because if we spend too much time planning this out, you might miss your big chance to get what you want!"

"Ok, bye mom! I love you!" Brooke kissed into the phone and hung up.

Chelsea took a sip of her water and looked up over the rim to see David smiling at her knowingly.

"Did you hear yourself, Chelsea?"

"Yep," she confirmed.

"What did you hear?" he asked.

Chelsea put down her water and let out a big sigh. "If I spend too much time planning this out, I'll miss *my* chance too," she said quietly.

"Yep," David teased.

"Will you excuse me?" Chelsea said, as she pushed her chair back. "I need to go see a man about a job."

"Don't forget the little people who helped you along the way!" David happily called after her.

David paid the bill and got back in his car. Just as he started the engine, his phone rang.

"Talk to me," he said easily.

"Hey, David, it's me, Lisa. How was the volunteer meeting? Did I miss anything important?"

"Hey backatcha. It was long. Mimi came and talked about the tag sale and—don't scream—she wants to do a bake sale with it," he reported.

"We've got to get something more exciting going on," Lisa

81

sighed. "I'm really afraid we're going to lose some volunteers if we don't think of something to get people's pulses racing."

"Lisa, you sound like Chelsea," David fussed. "Listen, if you don't like it, do something about it."

"Yeah, yeah, okay," Lisa said. "So did you hear from Ted?"

"Yes. He told me all about RESOURCES and emailed me an example of how to do it. I'll tell you about it tomorrow," David said as he was turning into his street.

"I can't wait, just tell me now," Lisa asked impatiently.

"Ok, basically RESOURCES are everything you need to be able to get what you truly want," David explained.

"You mean like money and stuff?" she asked.

"Yes, money, time, health, skills and most importantly, people to help you," David explained. "Ted said that's really key. So if there's something you can't do because you don't know how or haven't got the time or whatever, you have to find someone to help you. Makes sense to me," he added.

"Makes sense to me too," Lisa said. "I'm all set on RESOURCES —except for a guy. I still need the guy part. It's no fun doing this alone."

"Do you need a guy to be *able* to get thin and open a dance studio, or is the guy more part of the DESIRE part?" David asked wisely.

"Ah, good point," Lisa said, "No, the guy is in the DESIRE part, definitely. I have the money I inherited from my grandmother, so I can afford to do it and I'll have plenty of time when I go part-time. You said you'd help me with the business plan and my brother said he'd co-manage it with me."

"Is anything missing?" David asked.

"Well, I'm not in any shape to teach dancing right now," Lisa confessed.

"Ok, so that's a RESOURCE that you'll need to get, right?" David asked carefully.

"If I'm really going to do this thing, I guess I'll have no choice, although the dieting thing still doesn't thrill me," Lisa admitted. "What about you? Are you all set on RESOURCES for the book?"

"All set," David responded, "but Chelsea wasn't. She said that the RESOURCE component was her missing link. We worked on it tonight and figured out her entire plan. She bolted out of here like a woman on a mission!"

"Cool!" Lisa exclaimed. "It would be fabulous if she actually got that job!"

"Hey, Lisa," David interjected, "I just pulled in my driveway, so let me go, okay?"

"Oh, sure no problem," she said with a strange tone.

"Are you okay, Lisa?" David asked.

"Yes, I'm fine David," she said unconvincingly.

"Do you need anything?" he probed.

"Nope. I'm good to go. Send me Ted's email, okay?" she asked.

"Will do," David confirmed. "Bye."

Lisa hung up without responding. David turned off his car and sat thinking about Lisa. Something was going on with her, but he had no idea what it could be.

83

FAST TRACK

Success is greatest when everyone works the Action Formula together.

- 8 -

Align Your Crew

David opened the garage door and walked into the kitchen. It was dead quiet and all the lights were out. *"Gil must be sleeping,"* he thought as he felt his way to the light switch.

When his eyes had adjusted to the bright fluorescent light, David noticed a notepad on the kitchen counter.

David -

I tried to call you but there must have been something wrong with your phone. My mom called and she's in the hospital. I'm taking a midnight flight. I'll call you from the airport. Don't worry.

I love you,
Me

David picked up the phone to call Gillian's cell but got her voice mail. "Hi it's me," he said into the phone. "I went for coffee after the meeting and I left my cell in the car. I'm sorry I missed you. Call me when you get in no matter what time it is. I'll be waiting up and if you want me to hop on a plane in the morning, just say the word and I will. In fact, I think I'm going to check on some flights now. Ok. Call me. I love you. Call me. Bye."

David hung up the phone and looked around the kitchen. It was so empty. How could a room feel so empty? He threw his coat down on the chair and walked into the living room. It was dark and cold and ... empty.

"What would I ever do if..." he cut off the thought quickly. It was incomprehensible that he would ever have to live without Gillian. Desperate for distraction, David went into the den and fumbled his way to the desk, knocking over something he

didn't recognize and feeling around until he found the switch on the lamp.

"One of these days I am going to install those clapper light things." It was a familiar refrain.

He pulled up his chair and opened his laptop to search for flights. "What am I doing? I don't even know if she's in Michigan or Florida." He decided to wait until she called and opened his email.

There was the usual spam, with offers to improve the performance of his car, his computer and every aspect of his body. Delete...delete...delete.

There was an email from the people who ran the author seminar, with a link to a follow-up, online training video. "I'll watch that at some point for sure," he promised himself, moving it into a folder with 17 other emails that had similar training links. He looked at the long list and sighed. There was plenty of time for that.

He began mentally reciting his litany of liabilities, "I'm never going to finish this book. Who am I kidding? I can't believe I threw away that money going to that seminar. I should just throw out this manuscript and stop torturing myself." Just then a window popped up with a chat invitation from Ted.

"Hey—good timing. I was just sitting here trashing myself," David confessed.

"Why, what's up?" Ted asked.

"I dunno. Can't seem to get going on this book."

"Oh I totally get that one. That was how I was about launching my new life before I learned the formula. I spent years resenting my life but I just couldn't get myself to take action to change it because I kept thinking about the down side—you know, things that could go wrong. I thought about the changes that I would have to make and how those would lead to other changes. Then I would think about Ruth and the kids and all the ways it would impact them and my heart would start pounding like I was running a marathon. Is that what you're doing?"

"Yeah—among other things. Mostly I just can't seem to make myself sit down and write the damned thing. I think maybe I need to go back and do those DESIRE questions you told me about."

"Definitely do that. In the meantime I might be able to help you with the self-mutilation you're doing."

"Whatcha got for me?"

"That night in Dallas, my tycoon friend reminded me of something I knew but had long forgotten and that is that every good thing has a *consequence* associated with it. Action only occurs when we're willing to accept the consequences of our potential failure or success. We have to give ourselves PERMISSION to change and accept the changes that come to our lives as a result."

"So what am I supposed to do—just say, 'I give myself PERMISSION' and then POOF! I'm a success?"

"That's exactly what I said when he told me about this. Great minds think alike and all that."

"Yeah so what did he say?"

"He said that he couldn't teach me how to get PERMISSION until I had aligned my crew."

"Huh?"

"We have to speak back to the critical voices that tell us we can't do something or shouldn't have something and find the voices that show us how to do it and that give us the strength of will to say 'no' to failure and 'yes' to success."

"Now you're sounding like a motivational speaker."

"Hey—don't shoot the messenger."

"Go on."

"He told me that I had to get to know the voices inside me that were blocking my success and forcing me to play by rules that didn't fit my goals."

"Did he tell you how to do that?"

"Yep!"

"Ok—this is good stuff. I'm going to see if Chelsea and Lisa are online and conference them in—hold on..."

David looked at his list and found that both women were online. He sent out invitations and they joined the chat.

"Hi guys! What's up?" Chelsea asked.

"Good evening one and all!" Lisa added.

"Ted is about to teach me about the PERMISSION piece of the formula and I thought you guys might want to hear it."

"You bet!" Lisa said.

"I'm in!" Chelsea responded.

"Ok folks," Ted began. "Now don't make me nuts with everyone talking at once. Just sit back and enjoy the ride."

"Action begins when you find all the voices inside you and get them working together like a finally tuned instrument. And don't tell me you don't talk to yourself, Lisa because I see you sitting there thinking *'I don't talk to myself, what's his problem?'*"

Lisa broke into a smile. "Busted! Ok, great Yoda of the Palm Trees. Bestow upon us your infinite wisdom."

"Hey—it's not *my* wisdom. This is straight from the horse's mouth. I just did what my new friend told me to do and it worked."

"So what about these voices?" David asked.

Ted continued. "All total, there are five voices and you need them all to work together to support you and help you get what you want. My guy said to think of these voices as **real people**

living inside us. Obviously," he chuckled, "they're very *small* people.

"The goal is to get all five of these inside people to work together like the crew of the finest sailing yacht. Otherwise you sail in circles and never get anywhere.

"I think that's what's happening to me," David confessed.

"Me too," Lisa chimed in.

"I understand," Ted confided. "At first, my Internal Crew was totally in conflict but once I figured it out, my crew came together like they were competing in the America's Cup Race and it was full speed ahead!

"So how'd you do it?" Chelsea asked.

"The first step is actually to listen to them and pay attention to what they're saying. Sometimes they'll sound like your own voice and other times they'll sound like people from your past. My Internal Crew's voices were all over the place—young, old, male, female—it was hard to keep track of them at first. But no matter what they sounded like, they always held the same five positions in my head just as my friend told me they would."

"So what are the five positions?" David asked.

Ted held up a picture in front of his web-cam. "Ok—Can everyone see this? These are the five Internal Crew members you have to get aligned."

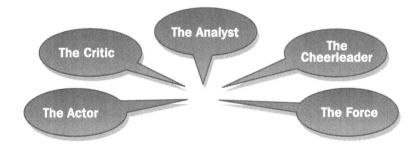

Chelsea leaned closer to the screen. "Wow! It's like that movie—what was it called?"

Lisa waved her arm as if she were competing in a game show. "Oh! Oh! Pick me! Pick me!" she begged.

"Yes, Lisa?" Chelsea giggled.

"*The Five Faces of Eve!*"

"That is absolutely correct!" Chelsea applauded. "You win a trip around the world, a brand new car and a lifetime supply of Stain-Be-Gone!"

"No wonder we can't get anything done on the Board," David laughed.

Ted threw his head back in laughter. "Listen you guys, I understand why you're laughing. When my Dallas guy first explained this to me I thought he was crazy. But the more details he gave me, the more I knew he was on to something big."

"Like what kind of details?" Chelsea asked.

"The specifics of the five Internal Crew Members and what they do to support and block our success," Ted explained,

"Well come on! Don't hold back on us now!" Lisa encouraged.

"Ok, we'll start with **The Critic.** He's the member of our Internal Crew that passes negative judgment about us and everyone else."

Ted pulled his chair back, put one hand on his hip and pointed the other at the screen. "You never do anything you say you're going to do. You're just a lazy, good for nothing..."

"AH! Stop! You sound like my mother!" Lisa screamed.

Ted wheeled himself back to the table. "Sorry Lis. I was just trying to show you what I mean."

"I think we got it, Ted, thanks," Lisa pouted.

"We've all got a Critic that looms above us all the time, prohibiting us from going after our DESIRES and placing stop signs and speed limits at every turn. Sometimes that can be a good thing because the Critic protects us from danger, so we need him to hang around. But we can't possibly succeed unless we have other crew members to counter his negative impact."

Lisa pretended to put her hands over her ears. "How do you turn him off?"

"Use your **Cheerleader.** He's our greatest ally against the Critic's negativity. He nurtures and encourages, cares for and supports us and others in our daily lives. The Cheerleader is a key player because he tells us to take risks, to try new things and to go after what we really want. The extent to which we have an effective Cheerleader determines whether we succeed in a change initiative—particularly when the going gets tough."

"Did you have a strong Cheerleader, Ted?" Chelsea asked.

"No, not really. In fact I'm still learning to develop that part of my crew. In the meantime, Ruth is my Cheerleader," Ted smiled.

"I can picture that perfectly," Chelsea nodded.

"So who's next?" David asked eagerly.

"**The Analyst.** This is the fact center of our Internal Crew. $2 + 2 = 4$. No emotion, no opinions, just logical strategizing and accurate computations. The Analyst shows us how to do things and figures out the RESOURCES we need in order to achieve our DESIRES. Without this member of our crew we could never figure out the roadmap to our destination, let alone get there."

"It's your Analyst that's teaching this to us now, right?" Chelsea asked.

"Yes, Chelsea, good job!"

"And that was your Cheerleader!" Lisa proudly added.

"I'm getting the hang of this!"

"Good for you Lisa!" Ted smiled. "Are you ready for the next one?"

Lisa bounced in her chair. "Yes!"

"The next member of your crew is incredibly powerful. He's called **'The Actor'** because he is the part of us that fakes it."

"You mean like 'fake it 'til you make it'?" Lisa asked.

"Sort of," Ted replied. "But the Actor fakes everything. He keeps us from saying what we think, being authentic with people and doing what we really want. When my friend told me about the Actor I figured I should just get rid of him from my crew but he reminded me that sometimes we need to be able to play by the rules."

"I think my Actor has saved me once or twice in our AACDA meetings," Lisa confessed. "Imagine if I told Mimi what I *really* think about her tag sales?"

Chelsea started giggling. "Or if I told Carl what I think of his guitar playing?"

"Yeah I think I'll hold onto mine too—but it sounds like you think there's a downside to this Actor," David noticed.

"My friend said that the Actor is one of the main reasons most people don't get what they want because the Actor's so busy following the rules he forgets to notice when the rules are getting in his way," Ted explained.

"So how are you supposed to know when to listen to your Actor and when to ignore him?" Chelsea asked.

"You call on the fifth member of your Internal Crew. This one is the most important of all. My friend called him **The Force.**"

"Now I feel like I just walked into a Star Wars movie," Lisa giggled.

Chelsea raised up her arm wielding her pen and pointed it at the screen. "Use the force, Luke!"

"Ok, ok, very funny. Maybe there's a reason they called this The Force in the movie. Because the fact is, this part of us is the core of our power and strength. He is the energy that drives us to action. The Force holds our creativity, our instincts and our passions. He feels deeply and dreams freely. Without the Force, our lives are meaningless and empty, without richness or connection or depth. He is the source of our DESIRES and my friend said that people who don't listen to their Forces rarely get what they truly want."

"I can't remember the last time I paid attention to what I really want," David confessed. "By the time I get up, go to work, do my AACDA stuff and come home, the only thing I can pay attention to is beer and bed."

"That's about where I was before Dallas. My friend said that most people are stuck in status quo because they don't pay attention to their Forces."

"So why don't we?" Lisa asked.

"I think most of us are taught to squash our Forces beginning from the first time an adult says *"Shush!"* As we grow older, more and more limits are placed on us and we're taught to conform to the cultural rules of our country, our institutions, our families and our peers. And while it all might have a cultural purpose and may even be necessary for the protection of our society as a whole, it also has an unintended result—it cramps our uniqueness and creativity and blocks us from being fully present and connected to others. It puts our Force in park and paves the way for our Actor to take the driver's seat."

"Wow. That's pretty sad, huh?" Chelsea remarked.

"So how does all of this come together for PERMISSION?" David asked.

"The normal process is that all five Internal Crew Members continually battle for control and the loser is us. The Force tries to break free but the Critic throws up a block while the Actor takes over and follows the rules in a learned desperation to toe the line. The Analyst keeps chugging along calculating and maneuvering while the Cheerleader encourages the entire Crew in a continuous, go-nowhere loop that perpetuates the status quo and blocks our success.

"The good news is that when we discover the right roadmap, all the Internal Crew Members start going in the same direction, in service of our DESIRES. At that point the five Internal Crew members come together to form a synergistic energy that is unstoppable. And that, my friends, is when we shatter our speed limits."

"Wait! That's the same thing you said the other day. What's up with this 'shatter our speed limits' thing?" David asked.

"I promise I'll explain that to you—but you've got to get the Internal Crew thing first or it won't make any sense."

"Ok, so how do we do that?" Chelsea asked.

"You just have to start paying attention to the voices in your head and get them talking to each other so they can work out the conflicts," Ted explained. "It took me a while to get it. I started experimenting with my family because I figured they'd love me even if I made a fool of myself. As it turned out, it was easy and now Ruth and the boys tell me I'm much better to be around. Now I focus on using my Cheerleader, my Analyst and my Force and only use the Critic and Actor when it fits my goal. I'm not perfect yet. Last night, my youngest left a soda can on the forward deck and my Critic came out in full force. God bless him, he looked up at me and said, *"Can I have a different member of your crew please?"* Broke me up, ya know?"

"Yeah, I know what you mean," Chelsea sighed. "I try to be careful about that with the girls but sometimes when I'm tired I think my Critic can be pretty lethal."

"I guess that was my Critic talking to me right before you called before," David admitted.

"So, what does all of this have to do with the Action Formula?" Lisa asked.

"Well, here's what my friend explained to me: He said as long as my Internal Crew was in conflict about which rules to follow, I would never get out of second gear to take action. And he was right. My Force was totally depressed and ready to quit my job, but my Actor kept telling me about how I had a responsibility to the company and my family to play by the rules and just keep going to that desk every day. My Analyst was the genius that came up with the idea for the second site so that I could get everything I wanted and not have to quit my job and my Cheerleader encouraged me to go for it. That got my Force all revved up and excited about getting everything I wanted and so I wrote it all out and then just as I was heading out the door to talk to Jason—CRASH! My Critic threw up a huge barricade telling me how I could never pull it off and would only send my family and the company into bankruptcy.

"I was going around in circles for a couple of days until I found a way to help all members of my Internal Crew reach a consensus. It turned out to be relatively simple—I just searched for the rules that my Critic and Actor were fighting so hard to sustain. After that, all I had to do was recruit my Force, Analyst and Cheerleader to break the rules that were keeping me from getting what I really wanted. Then I created new rules that propelled me forward in record-breaking time. Done.

"You make it sound easy," David said.

"It was!" Ted smiled.

"So much for psychotherapy," Lisa laughed.

"Hey therapy is great for a lot of people. But this worked for me faster than any therapy I've ever had or heard of," Ted explained. "Of course, I had my friend to coach me through it, so I guess that was sort of like having a therapist. All I know is it worked and it worked fast."

"So how did you get from that to living in Paradise?" Chelsea asked.

"I started using the Internal Crew concept at work. I taught all of my team members about their Internal Crews and helped them to find the PERMISSION to make critical changes so they could break industry standards for excellence. I showed them how to find their personal DESIRES for success and how to discover the missing RESOURCES they needed to be able to make it happen. The results were measurable. In fact, since we got down here, we've broken every projection. We're not only ahead of schedule we're coming in under budget.

"It's all Monday morning quarterbacking, but when I think about the way I led my team for all those years, it's amazing to me that we did as well as we did. Now that I see how much more productive everyone is and how much more collegial our team has become—my Critic wants to kick me for all the time we lost. All I had to do was use my Internal Crew in a strategic manner to align all the Internal Crews of my people—the end result was a powerful, unstoppable team.

"I'm sure you're thinking I've gone all touchy-feely, psychobabble on you guys, but believe me, I'm still the same guy I've always been. The difference is that now, I'm my own guy. Nobody tells me what I can and can't do in my life. Now nobody makes my rules but ME. I like my rules much better. I'm not hurting anyone and I'm not doing anything illegal."

"So what are these rules you keep talking about?" David

asked.

"I'll tell you what. Ruth is bringing a surprise lunch for my team here and she'll be here any minute. How about you guys work on the Internal Crew for a while and I'll catch up with you later?"

"Sounds good. Thanks Ted!" Lisa said.

"Yes, really, Ted, thank you!" Chelsea added.

"I'll talk to you tomorrow, buddy. Good night ladies," David said.

As everyone clicked off, David leaned back in his chair and thought about everything Ted had told them.

"Five Internal Crew members? Just what I need—five more mouths to feed," he thought, smiling at his own joke. He was definitely his own best audience.

He listened for the little people inside of him, but all he heard was water gurgling through the baseboard as the heat filled the room. The sound lulled him into a hypnotic trance as his eyelids got heavy and his head started to bob, *"I definitely have a Critic on my crew,"* he thought, just as his head dropped down onto his shoulder. The next thing he knew it was 2:15 a.m. and the phone had awakened him with a start.

He lunged for the receiver and started speaking immediately. "Are you ok?" he said frantically, "How's your mom? Where are you? Do you want me to come?" He couldn't get the questions out fast enough.

"I'm fine and she's fine," Gillian reported. "It turned out to be something minor. I can tell you about it in the morning, but it really scared us. They're going to keep her overnight and I'm going to stay out here with her for a few days."

"Yes, okay, no problem," David confirmed. "Do you want me to come out? Where are you anyway?"

"Miami," she said yawning.

"You must be beat," David said softly.

"I am. I'll go back to her place and catch some sleep but I wanted to call you before it got too much later. Are you okay?" She habitually worried about him and everyone in her life.

"Gil, do you think I'm critical and stuck behind a bunch of rules?" David asked.

"What?!" Gillian sounded totally shocked. "What are you talking about?"

"It's nothing," David said. "Forget it."

"David, listen to me," she commanded. "You are a brilliant man and you will do that book when you're ready and it will be a best seller. I love you and we'll be fine no matter what. Got it?"

"Got it," he laughed. "You're my best cheerleader, Gil. I don't know what I'd do without you."

"You'll never have to know, honey." She yawned into the phone. "I'm sorry but I've *got* to go to bed."

"Ok, I love you," David said quietly.

"Me too on you," Gillian replied. "Good night."

David hung up the phone and shut down his laptop.

"Ok, Internal Crew, let's go to bed." He laughed to himself as he turned off the light and walked up the stairs to go to bed. *"I wouldn't mind meeting that Force,"* he thought, *"He sounds pretty cool."*

As soon as David laid his head down his eyes popped wide open. He stared into the darkness and thought about Ted. *"I wouldn't mind seeing those rules of his too. I bet he had some good ones."*

- 9 -

Take Charge

David spent the morning on the phone with clients and then drove downtown to the trade show to check on his booth and see how his team was doing. He often made unannounced visits in the field and his team welcomed his support. As he walked into the enormous showroom, he noticed his assistant and started over to the booth just in time to hear her yelling at a convention center employee.

"Where's our banner? Why isn't it up?" she screamed, placing her hands on her hips. "How could you guys be so careless? Do you know what time it is?" she fussed, tapping her watch and shaking her head with disgust.

"Wow," David thought, *"The Critic That Ate Manhattan."* He walked up to her and quietly asked, "Christie, may I speak with you please?"

"David, I'm sorry about this," she said sweetly. "I know it's important that we follow the guidelines and specifications to get this done the way you want it, but things are a little behind schedule today."

David started to smile as he realized that he had just met Christie's Actor. He was intrigued and decided it might be fun to find the other members of her Internal Crew.

"So Christie, what time do you think it will be done?" he asked unemotionally.

"Well, it is currently 9:05," she said, matter-of-factly, "It will take us approximately 30 minutes to finish the electric and then we'll be all set."

David smiled, thinking, *"Analyst, check. Ok, I'll follow Ted's advice and use my Cheerleader and Force to see if I can get that out of her too..."*

"Hey Christie," he said. "I am so excited about this booth. I think we have the potential to blow the roof off this place today and you're just the woman to make it happen! Sure, we're running late, but I have total confidence in you that you're going to find a way to get it moving."

"Thanks, David," Christie beamed. If she'd been a peacock, her feathers would have fluffed up and out.

"Why don't you grab some coffee and bring it over to the workmen. Maybe you can do a cheerleader routine and get them moving faster," David suggested.

"Good idea!" Christie said gleefully. She grabbed an empty box, carefully placed three Styrofoam cups of coffee inside and practically skipped back to the booth. David watched her set it just right so it wouldn't spill, then bring a cup over to a man standing on the ladder nearest their booth.

"Hi Jerry!" she said. "I brought you some coffee. Sorry about the Queen Bitch of the Amazon thing before. I don't know what came over me. You guys are doing an awesome job and if anyone can get us up and running, it's you. Let me know if you need anything. I'll just be right over here out of your way."

The man looked down at her, smiled and said, "Don't worry, Christie. We'll do your electric first and have this up and ready in ten minutes tops."

"Ok," thought David, *"Now I'm impressed."*

"Good job, Christie!" David offered, "I'll see you back at the office. Clearly you've got your crew under control."

"This Internal Crew thing isn't so hard," he thought as he walked back to his car and opened his door locks with the remote.

"So if you're so smart, why haven't you finished your book?"

David looked around for a quick second, but no one was there.

"Oh," he thought as he suddenly recognized his own Critic.

"You never finish anything you say you're going to do," the Critic continued. *"In fact, you're the world's greatest procrastinator. What about that clapper light thing? And Gillian's shelves? And you still haven't programmed the speed dial on your cell phone!"*

"I've been a little busy," he defended silently. He got in the car, closed the door and said out loud, "Ok, now listen: I'm in charge here and I want a burger and then we're going back to the office to finish the month-end report before we go to the Board meeting tonight. Anybody got a problem with that?"

He turned on the radio to block out any response and began to wonder if he was losing it.

- 10 -

Lock In
Your
Permissions

"I just heard that my meeting is canceled tonight and Gillian is still at her mom's. Do you want to go grab dinner after work?" David said into the phone.

"Sure, I never turn down a meal," Lisa said. "What's Chelsea doing?"

"I don't know. I called you first. Can you call her? I'm swamped here," David mumbled as he shuffled through papers.

"Yeah, sure. No problem. I'll see you at the Corner Café. Six o'clock ok?" Lisa asked.

"Perfect," replied David. "See you then."

David finished his work by 5:00 and since it was far too early to leave, he decided to send an email to Ted.

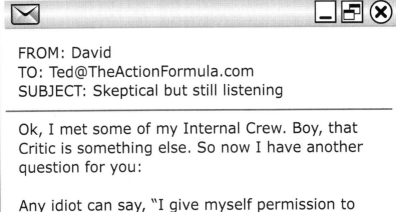

FROM: David
TO: Ted@TheActionFormula.com
SUBJECT: Skeptical but still listening

Ok, I met some of my Internal Crew. Boy, that Critic is something else. So now I have another question for you:

Any idiot can say, "I give myself permission to succeed," but that's not going to cut it when the road starts curving and the grade gets steeper.

Frankly, Ted, it seems like motivational hoo-hah. You know—just keep saying positive affirmations to yourself until you get brainwashed. Not that there's anything wrong with that—but it doesn't work all the time for everyone, ya know?

Am I missing something here? Speak to me, oh
Yoda of the Tropics. What's with the rules thing?

Signed,
Your Faithful (if somewhat skeptical) Follower

He sat staring into space until he heard a pop from his computer. Ted was awake and ready to talk.

"Ok, whatcha got for me, big guy?" he wondered as he accepted Ted's invitation.

"What are you doing awake at this hour?" David asked.

"We're testing the new systems today and I wanted to get a jump start before everyone gets in here. I have a lot more drive to get it right—now that I'm in charge."

"Makes total sense. So did you get my email?"

"Yeah—I think I'm liking this 'faithful follower' thing." Ted leaned back in his chair and took a sip from his mug. "This island coffee is amazing. I'll have to send some back to you."

"Sounds good. Listen, I'm totally confused about this PERMISSION thing. I've got the Internal Crew but I still don't get how this fits in with the Action Formula."

"I know. I'm not as good a teacher as my dinner partner. Maybe if I tell you how I used what he taught me it'll make more sense to you."

"Give it a shot."

"When I got back from Dallas I went in to work the next day. I was sitting there trying to find my way through the mess that had accumulated when Chuck came in to deliver the mail. You don't know him, but just look in your mailroom: You've got a 'Chuck,' too."

David smiled. "Yes, we do."

"So Chuck had been doing our company mail for as long as I could remember, and never complained, never asked for a raise, just kept doing the same thing every day—and he seemed to be perfectly happy doing it.

"I asked him if it ever bothered him, doing the same thing day in and day out and he said—you're gonna love this—'*My mother taught me that doing the same thing, the same way, every day will guarantee me a place in Heaven.*'"

"My mother taught me? Oh, come on, Ted, that's really what he said?"

Ted raised his hand as if taking an oath. "I swear to you on a stack, buddy."

"So what'd you do?"

"I didn't do anything. I just sat there staring at him and then suddenly I understood exactly what my friend had told me."

"What's that?"

"All of our major choices in life are based on rules we adopt before we know any better."

"What did he mean by that?"

"He meant that everything we do—every choice we make—every decision we make—every opinion we hold is based on things we learned before we had enough experience to know any better. When I saw Chuck I realized my friend was absolutely right.

"I looked around my office and saw it through different eyes. It was an exact replica of the one my grandfather had at the factory when I was growing up. Then I looked at myself. My socks matched my pants (got that from Dad) and my pants were perfectly creased (thanks to Mom).

David instinctively checked his socks and pants. They were fine. "Go on."

"I looked at my calendar and saw that I had no vacations scheduled for the entire year. One of my MBA mentors taught me that. Then my eye caught the clock and it was noon so I got up to go to lunch—until I realized I really wasn't hungry. I was only going to lunch because, somewhere along the line, someone told me I'm *supposed* to eat lunch at noon."

"I do that all that time."

"I'm telling you David, it was like I saw this complete movie of my life with subtitles, and all of the subtitles were rules that I had learned along the way. Every single one of those rules explained why I was sitting where I was at that moment in my heavily starched shirt and perfectly knotted tie.

"I went home that weekend and spent all day Saturday with a legal pad. I wrote down every rule I had ever learned, going back to as early as I could remember. I pictured grade school and holiday dinners, fights with my friends and embarrassing times in gym classes. I carried it through college and grad school, into my work life and even into my marriage."

"Like what kind of rules?"

"Rules about what TO DO and rules about what NOT TO DO, what to THINK and what NOT TO THINK, about what to FEEL and what NOT TO FEEL, about who to BE and who NOT TO BE."

"I can't picture this. Give me some examples."

"Well, some of my rules had been taught to me verbally like "Don't talk in the movies" and "Be a good boy" and "Clean your plate" and "Be like your brother.""

"Oh I get it. Like when my mom used to tell us 'Sit up straight!' or when my teacher used to say 'Stay within the lines, David.' Oh that made me nuts!"

"Right. And it wasn't just the rules they told us out loud. In fact, most of the rules we learn we got just by watching people around us. Their rules become ours. Like when I was in grad school I had a professor who always closed his eyes before he answered. I thought that was so cool because I read it as 'Think before you speak.' To this day, I still close my eyes and think long and hard before I answer. Drives Ruth crazy."

David laughed. "I'm sure I've got a few of those that rattle Gillian's cage. But what does this have to do with PERMISSION?"

"Our rules all come together like an enormous script in a play and then our Actors assume the roles and follow the rules to perfection."

"So then—that means what exactly?"

"It means that your Force doesn't get a say in the matter. What if I wanted to be a guest on a radio talk show? I'll never be able to pull that off as long as I have a rule that I have to close my eyes and think long and hard before I answer."

"You want to be on a radio talk show?"

"No, that was just an example. Ok, try this. I'm going to send you my list of rules and when you look at them you'll see exactly what I'm talking about. Wait a minute..."

David watched as Ted fed yellow paper into his scanner. "I'm sending you my original notes. They're kind of scratchy, but you'll get the idea."

"Tell me this technology thing isn't cool," David smiled.

"I know—never ceases to amaze me. Ok, you should be getting it soon."

"Yep. It just got here." David opened the email attachment and looked at Ted's list.

Ted's Old Rules

Do Rules

1. Be perfect
2. Be strong
3. Try hard
4. Be on time
5. Please people
6. Be sad
7. Be angry
8. Be careful
9. Be a good boy
10. Be what I want you to be
11. Be just like me
12. Be just like your brother
13. Be a success
14. Be a planner
15. Be a good husband and father
16. Suffer in silence
17. Clean your plate
18. Forgive everyone but you
19. Stay busy
20. Make the best of it
21. Be in control
22. Work hard
23. Study hard
24. Play hard
25. Be thoughtful
26. Take care of your family
27. Kiss your wife every day
28. Read to your children
29. Smack your kid
30. Stay on top of things
31. Be responsible
32. Look your best
33. Obey the rules
34. Do the right thing

Don't Rules

1. Don't make mistakes
2. Don't fail
3. Don't trust
4. Don't be a kid
5. Don't play
6. Don't talk to strangers
7. Don't talk back
8. Don't stick up for yourself
9. Don't say "no"
10. Don't trust yourself
11. Don't ask for help
12. Don't do what you want
13. Don't get close to people
14. Don't have fun
15. Don't express feelings
16. Don't ask for anything
17. Don't break the rules
18. Don't talk in movies
19. Don't break family traditions

"Wow."

"See what I mean?"

"There's a ton of 'em!"

"I know. And that's not even all of them. When I first got them all down on paper I didn't like what I saw. In fact, I got really pissed. I couldn't believe I'd been living all those rules for all these years and never knew it. Talk about your self-imposed prison!"

"But that wasn't your fault. You were just doing what we all do."

"Exactly. I'd taken on the script that was handed to me by my culture's elders. It wasn't their fault either. They were only doing what they had been taught. No one was to blame. But now it was time to break tradition and create my own rules."

"You know, Ted, I remember once when I was in college I came home complaining about something and my mom looked me straight in the eyes and said, *"David, if you don't like it, change it."* David's voice cracked. "Sorry, I still get a little choked up about that."

"I understand buddy. Need a minute?"

"Nah—I'm fine. Go on."

"So I took this list and went over it one rule at a time. Some of my rules sounded pretty good until I realized that they were rules and that meant I had no choice but to follow them. Like, see the one that says *Work Hard?*"

"Yeah. That's a good rule, right? I mean, shouldn't we all work hard?"

"Well, you'd think so. Except, when you think about it, it's a *rule.* So that means you're never allowed to *not* work hard. That was me. Even when I was playing tennis, I was working really hard at it. I never could just chill and enjoy the game."

"Oh, I see what you mean."

FAST TRACK

All of our major choices in life are based on rules we adopt before we know any better.

"And then there was *Be strong.* Well, come on! All men want to be strong. That's a keeper. But then I remembered my dad's funeral. My mom was really broken up about dad's death and so I figured I had to be strong for her. Ten years later, sitting in my chair, I realized I still hadn't cried. It seemed like there was something really wrong with that. My dad was a good man and he deserved my tears."

"Damn right. So what'd you do?"

"I remembered what the Dallas guy told me. He said I should go through all my rules and change the ones that were blocking my success. So I looked at this list and realized I had to change these rules or they were going to send me to an early grave.

"I started to cross them off, one at a time until I'd eliminated all the rules that were keeping me from getting what I wanted. There were a lot of them. When I'd finished my list, it was like the first time you switch from regular gas to racing fuel... instant velocity. The next thing I knew I had created a life that was filled with everything I'd ever wanted. It was just that fast.

"It was weird. I mean, I could actually feel my Force getting bigger inside me and I became so excited I had to jump up and show my list to Ruth. She was impressed, but skeptical and gave me one of her *Well, we'll have to see how long this lasts* looks." Ted scrunched his mouth and raised his right eyebrow to show David 'the look.'

"I hate those looks."

"Me too. Anyway, about a week later, I fell off the wagon. One of the rules on my old list was Be Perfect. I had decided to get rid of that rule and replaced it with *It's okay to make mistakes now and then.* Well, everything was going pretty smoothly—until I actually made a mistake."

"Oops."

Ted's New Rules

1. I can make mistakes now and then
2. I don't have to be strong all the time
3. I always do my best
4. I'll help people whenever I can
5. I can be whatever I want to be
6. I'll ask for help when I need it or want it
7. I'll forgive others
8. I'll forgive myself
9. I'll be thoughtful of others' needs
10. I'll do my best to stay on top of things. and if something falls through the cracks. I'll re-read rule # 1
11. I'll look my best at least once a week
12. It's ok to break the rules if the rules are hurting me or my family
13. I'll let myself have fun
14. I'll express my emotions freely
15. I'll listen to my Force and trust it
16. I'll let myself be successful and enjoy my success
17. I'll let myself change
18. I'll follow my new rules starting right now

"Yeah—big oops. I was in the garage changing my oil and knocked over a full bottle and it went everywhere. Well, out came the old Ted. I threw a flashlight across the garage and broke the thing into a thousand little pieces and scared Ruth half out of her skin.

"She had the good sense not to push it at the time, but we both knew what had happened. I'd gone back to my old rule and was ashamed that I had made that mistake. My shame came out in full-blown rage.

"The next weekend I took out the old list again. There were just too many to keep track of, so I tried a different approach. I looked at all my old rules and tried to summarize all of them into just one rule. I figured if I could find that one rule then I could break it and unravel the entire script like a Gordian knot."

"Good idea. Did it work?"

"Nope. At least not at first. I came up with all kinds of ideas but nothing that really fit. The next day I was in the middle of the sixth Fairway at Ridgewood, playing with a few clients, and I hooked that ball something fierce and sent it way off into the woods. As I reached into my bag for another ball, I heard my Critic loud and clear: *You loser! You're not good enough to be playing with these guys.*"

"Whoa—that's pretty rough."

"Yeah but that's when it hit me. I'd heard that line thousands of times in my life. In fact, I couldn't remember a time when I didn't hear that in my head. It was like an old familiar ache and it explained everything. *I'm not good enough.*"

Ted turned his head away from the screen and David leaned in. "Are you okay?"

"I'm fine. Look, this is a little embarrassing for me, but I'm going to give you some background so it will all make sense. I'd appreciate it if you wouldn't let the girls in on this one, okay?"

David mimed a zipper on his mouth.

"Ok, David, that's just a little grade school, don't you think?"

115

"Just trying to lighten things up a little."

"No, not this time, buddy. This is serious stuff."

"Sorry Ted. Don't worry, I won't tell anyone."

"Ok. Well, when I was in sixth grade I flunked a math test. It was an important one and I had to bring it home for my parents' signatures. I tried to fake my way through it and tell them that it was no big deal, but Dad was big time mad and the next thing I knew he had me in a vice grip, nose-to-nose yelling, *"You're not good enough to eat at my table... You'll never amount to anything... How could you do this to your mother?"* Clearly stuff he learned in Good Parenting Class.

"I stood there frozen, listening to him yell, and looked over at Mom for some kind of reprieve. She just gave me 'the look' and turned away and I was totally confused. They'd never acted like that before. I tried to figure out why it was all happening. Why I'd flunked the test, why Dad was yelling, and why Mom was so ashamed. And then it hit me. Dad was right. *I wasn't good enough.*"

"Oh, man."

"I came to believe that about myself completely and used it to explain everything that went wrong, everything I was afraid to try and everything I couldn't master. It became my GUIDING RULE. Obviously I had other rules that balanced it, or I wouldn't have gotten as far as I did in life. But when I pushed it to the limit by entertaining the idea of opening my own business, my GUIDING RULE kicked in—proof positive that my Actor should keep on playing the role of CFO. That way, the world would never find out the truth about me: that I just wasn't good enough to build my own business and be a success."

"That makes total sense."

"My Dallas guy said we all have rules that we make in

response to stressful situations. At the time, we don't realize they're rules. They're more like conclusions or decisions that help us deal with a difficult moment. But then every time we come up against anything in our life that remotely resembles that moment, we revert back to our original decision until it becomes a GUIDING RULE that we use to explain every roadblock along the way."

"I get it now. But is there only one GUIDING RULE?"

"No, there can be a bunch of them, depending on how many difficult situations we've encountered along the way. Each rule blocks our success in some way because we simply accept the logic of the situation rather than try to find a way around each barricade. Our GUIDING RULES explain it all so that there is no point in fighting the good fight because we completely believe that it's a fight we can't win."

"Over the course of our lives, we make all of our major decisions based on our GUIDING RULES, but this is no more a conscious process than driving a car. Once you learn how to drive, you don't have to think about all the rules. You go on automatic."

Ted shook his head in disbelief. *"I'm not good enough.* I'd been living my life based on this rule and I knew instinctively that since I'd already figured out my RESOURCES, this was the only thing blocking the road between me and my DESIRES."

David was at the edge of his seat. "So how'd you get away from it? I mean, if it's a GUIDING RULE how do you break it?"

"I said it over and over in my head. I just couldn't stop saying it. And then out of the blue I heard my Cheerleader say, *"That's ridiculous! You're not that same kid any more! You're CFO of one of the largest shipping companies in the world.*

117

You're a good father, a loving husband, you have great friends, and you give back every chance you get."

"Cool!"

"And then I heard another voice—one I hadn't heard in a long time. At first it was kind of small and quiet. And then it got louder and stronger until I couldn't possibly ignore it."

David was so excited he couldn't stand himself. "Who?!"

"My Force. It started out so soft I could barely hear it, but then I heard him loud and clear: *I am totally good enough and I always was. In fact, I can do anything I set my mind to do."*

"Good for you, Ted!"

"David, I'm telling you I've never felt anything like that. Powerful and excited and hopeful and free! It was like the fog lifted and I could see the world more clearly. Does that sound corny to you?"

"Well, maybe a little."

"Well, it wasn't corny to me. It made perfect sense. This was the missing piece of the formula for me, my PERMISSION. I decided to make it my NEW GUIDING RULE: *I am totally good enough and I always was and I can do anything I set my mind to do!"*

"Now that's not corny at all."

"No—it was exactly the ticket I needed to get on the fast track. I made a commitment to live my new rule and without even trying all the other rules just seemed to get broken. My entire script unraveled and I was free. I mean really free."

"Sounds awesome."

"It was exactly the way my Dallas friend said it would be. As soon as I had my NEW GUIDING RULE, I was ready to launch. I trotted into Jason's office and sold him my idea with a plan to be up and running in 6 months. He gave me the green light and I sprung to action. In fact, I moved faster than I'd ever moved in my entire life. Decisions came quickly and tasks got done in record-breaking speed. I was on top of the world—for the first time in years. For that matter, so were our shareholders.

> ## Ted's Old Guiding Rule:
> I'm not good enough
>
> ## Ted's New Guiding Rule:
> I'm TOTALLY GOOD ENOUGH AND ALWAYS WAS!
> I CAN DO ANYTHING I SET MY MIND TO DO!

"The next thing I knew I was here with everything I wanted—freedom, independence, palm trees, time with my family, a kick-butt boat and a chance to prove to myself once and for all that I was good enough to do anything I wanted to do. I had shattered my speed limits and I was ready to go full speed ahead."

"That's what it means to shatter your speed limits? It means you break your rules?"

"That's the last piece of it, yes. To shatter your speed limits you need to: **Discover your Deepest DESIRES, Gather all your RESOURCES and Lock in your PERMISSION."**

"Ok, now I get it. So talk me through this PERMISSION thing one more time."

"Ok. Bottom line: **PERMISSION involves three steps:**

"1. Make a list of the rules you've learned in your life. You can use my list as a starting point to jog your thinking. And

remember—if people tried to teach you rules that you didn't agree with, they still count because your Actor knew you were supposed to follow them so they would have niggled at you any time you tried to go against them.

"2. Find your GUIDING RULE by <u>summarizing</u> all your old rules.
Remember, the GUIDING RULE doesn't have to be logical. It only has to be familiar. Something you've thought many times in your life. If you can't think of it, check out the second attachment I sent you in my email earlier. It's a list of some of the most common GUIDING RULES and it might jog your memory.

"3. Make a NEW GUIDING RULE that will free you from all of your old rules and give you the PERMISSION you need to take ACTION!

"Does that all make sense to you, David?"
"Totally. Hey Ted, thanks a bunch."
"No sweat, buddy. Glad to help. I've got to run. Like I said, this is a big day for us and if all goes well, we'll be three months ahead of schedule and celebrating big time!"
"Good luck! Let me know how it goes."
"Backatcha!"

Common Guiding Rules:

I'm not good enough
There's something wrong with me
I'll just settle for what I've got
I'll keep my mouth shut and my head down
I'll show you even if it kills me
I'll prove it to you
I'll never amount to anything
I'm a loser
I'm not worthy
I never get what I want
I'm not supposed to be happy
I'm a failure
I'll never make it
I'm just average
I have to work hard my entire life
I won't get close so I don't get hurt
I'll try harder
I have to be strong
Nobody likes me
I can't do anything right
I'll run away
I won't and you can't make me!
There's nothing I can do
I have to take care of her/him
It's my job to make you happy
I'm not smart enough
I can't make it on my own
I have to make it on my own
I don't need anybody
I'll never trust anybody
I have to keep my guard up
I'm different
I have no choice
I don't trust myself

To Find Your Permission

PERMISSION involves three steps:

1. Make a list of the rules you've learned in your life.

2. Find your GUIDING RULE by summarizing all your old rules.

3. Make a NEW GUIDING RULE that will free you from all of your old rules and give you the PERMISSION you need to take ACTION!

- 11 -
Choose Your Own Rules

By the time David had finished talking with Ted it was six o'clock and time to meet Chelsea and Lisa for dinner. He turned off his computer and looked out his office window at the gray sky. There was a snow advisory for the day and a warning for that evening.

He picked up his briefcase, locked the door behind him and went downstairs. Most of the city had shut down for the weekend and it was unusually quiet on the streets as he drove to the Corner Café. When he arrived, he found Lisa sitting alone in the corner.

Taking a seat, he asked, "Where's Chelsea?"

Lisa looked up from studying the menu. "She just texted me. Said she's going to be late and that we should start without her."

David looked up at the specials on the wall. "What looks good to you?"

Lisa stared up at the menu again as if for the first time. "A cheeseburger...And fries—no, wait—onion rings! And maybe even a hot fudge sundae!"

"Are we feeling a little self-indulgent?" David teased.

"Come on, David, humor me. I've been looking at perfectly sculptured bodies for an entire week and I want to spend the rest of the evening sabotaging my chances of ever looking that good. Help me out, huh?" she begged.

"What are you talking about?" he said. "Where are you finding perfectly sculptured bodies?"

"I've been watching my old dance videos trying to get motivated to do this studio thing. So far I can't make myself do it," Lisa sighed.

David thought about Ted. "You know, Lis, it may be a PERMISSION thing."

"What do you mean?" she asked, not sounding at all interested.

"Lisa, if you don't want to talk about this, it's really okay with me. We've been friends a long time and I love you no matter what. There's no law that says you have to do this. It's different for Chelsea and me. Our DESIRES aren't as personal as yours."

"You're wrong, David. Chelsea's promotion is just as important to her as my appearance is to me. And it doesn't *get* any more personal than writing a book!" We don't have any right to decide whose DESIRE is better or more important than someone else's."

"How'd you get so smart, huh?" David asked as he leaned over to mess up her hair.

She quickly put her hair back where it had been. "So, did you talk to Ted?"

"I just finished talking to him."

"What'd he have to say?"

"Well, he said that PERMISSION comes when we break through the rules that keep us from letting ourselves have what we truly want," David explained.

"Like what kind of rules?"

David took out the list of rules that Ted had sent to him.

"Do's and Don'ts that we learn growing up—and into our adult lives. Ted said you're supposed to look back over your life and write down all the rules you've learned along the way. When you identify all the little rules, you'll discover a big GUIDING RULE that is keeping you from taking action on your DESIRE." David turned the paper toward Lisa. "See? This is Ted's list."

Lisa looked at the list for a minute then looked up at David with really wide eyes.

"I don't think I ever realized Ted had so many rules!" she said.

"Yeah. It explains a lot, doesn't it?" David said.

"It's so funny, because this is totally Ted!" Lisa said amazed. She had a strange, distant look about her.

"What is it, Lisa?" David asked.

Lisa looked up at him and he saw the familiar red blotches on her neck. She called them her "stress meters." When the blotches came, Lisa was usually nervous about something.

"Lisa?" David pressed. He was getting a little worried.

"David, I think these rules describe me too," she said. "Only not exactly all of them," she added thoughtfully.

David handed her a pen. "Here—cross off the ones that don't fit for you."

Lisa did as David suggested. She knew immediately which fit and which didn't.

"Are there rules that you've been living that aren't on that list?" David asked.

"Yeah, there really are," Lisa said, "should I add them in?"

"You want to tell them to me and I'll write for you?" David offered.

"No thanks, I can do it." She said bravely. Slowly and methodically, she started to write.

Be nice
Be different
Be quiet
Be friendly
Don't rock the boat

"This is actually kind of fun!" Lisa exclaimed. "I keep picturing my family in my kitchen when I was about eight. It's amazing how easy it is to revisit old memories and translate them into the rules we were living."

"Are there more?" David asked.

"Oh I'm sure there are. How far back am I supposed to go?" she asked.

"Ted said that he looked at his life from childhood all the way through grad school and into his career."

"Oh, well, then I'd have to add things like

Be thin
Be sexy
Be rich
Be healthy
Don't eat carbs
Don't date your girlfriends' ex-boyfriends

"Huh?" David asked.

"It's a girl thing" she replied with a knowing smile.

She looked at her list. "Ok, that's good. Now what do I do?"

"Now you're supposed to find your GUIDING RULE," David instructed.

"My what?"

"Look at the whole list of your rules and come up with one summary rule that covers all of the rules you've written down." David explained. "Ted calls that the GUIDING RULE. He says that this is the rule that serves as the biggest barricade between DESIRE and PERMISSION"

"Wow. Ok, let's see" she said. "Here—look with me. What do you see, David?"

Ted's Old Rules

Do Rules

1. Be perfect
2. Be strong
3. Try hard
4. Be on time
5. Please people
6. Be sad
7. ~~Be angry~~
8. Be careful
9. Be a good ~~boy~~ girl
10. Be what I want you to be
11. Be just like me
12. ~~Be just like your brother~~
13. ~~Be a success~~
14. Be a planner
15. Be a good ~~husband and father~~ wife & mom
16. Suffer in silence
17. Clean your plate
18. Forgive everyone but you
19. Stay busy
20. Make the best of it
21. Be in control
22. Work hard
23. Study hard
24. Play hard
25. Be thoughtful
26. Take care of your family
27. ~~Kiss your wife every day~~
28. Read to your children
29. ~~Smack your kid~~
30. Stay on top of things
31. Be responsible
32. Look your best
33. Obey the rules
34. Do the right thing Be nice, Be different Be quiet, Be friendly Be thin, Be sexy Be rich, Be healthy

Don't Rules

1. Don't make mistakes
2. Don't fail
3. ~~Don't trust~~
4. ~~Don't be a kid~~
5. ~~Don't play~~
6. Don't talk to strangers
7. ~~Don't talk back~~
8. Don't stick up for yourself
9. Don't say "no"
10. Don't trust yourself
11. ~~Don't ask for help~~
12. Don't do what you want
13. Don't get close to people
14. ~~Don't have fun~~
15. ~~Don't express feelings~~
16. Don't ask for anything
17. Don't break the rules
18. ~~Don't talk in movies~~
19. Don't break family traditions

Guiding Rule

~~I'm not good enough~~

Don't rock the boat
Don't eat carbs
Don't date your girlfriends?
ex-boyfriends

"No, Lisa. You have to do this one. Ted said it'll come to you and it'll feel like an old, familiar ache when you hear it in your head," he explained. "Don't worry about me, I'll just sit here and eat my burger. You go ahead," he said warmly, "Just let me know if you get stuck...Oh wait...Ted gave me a sheet of common GUIDING RULES that you can use to jog your memory. Do you want to see it?"

"No, I'd rather try to figure this out on my own first." Lisa's voice trailed off as she began to look over her list. As she read her rules, she started to remember scenes from grade school, high school and finally college. She saw herself at her first audition for the City Ballet, then backstage and dancing in countless productions. She found herself looking into the eyes of people she hadn't seen in years and sorting through memories that she'd long ago filed away. It all happened in rapid motion, as each rule uncovered a host of memories.

Wrapped up in her thoughts, Lisa absently bit into her burger. As she started to chew it, something tasted wrong. She pulled back and looked at it. It wasn't a burger. It was a fried chicken patty wrapped in some kind of cheesy mess.

"What's wrong?" David asked, happily chewing his dinner.

"They gave me some chicken concoction," she answered, as she put it down on her plate.

"Oh, that's gross. Just send it back." David urged.

"No, that's ok," she said, "I don't want to complain. I'll just settle for what I got."

David stopped mid-bite. He was afraid to move. He wasn't sure if Lisa had heard what she'd just said. But as soon as she said it, David knew immediately. He'd heard her say it for years. It was her GUIDING RULE. He looked at her very carefully.

Lisa looked up and the two locked eyes.

"Holy crap!" she said excitedly, "I say that all the time, don't I?"

David started to answer, but she cut him off.

"I do! I do! I say that all that time! *'I'll just settle for what I got.'* And I know where I got it from too! Whenever we were getting ready for the new school year, Mom would take us shopping. She would buy my sister, Erica, new clothes, and she'd buy me new *shoes*. I'd ask her for new clothes and she would always say I had to wear Erica's clothes from the previous year. Of course I would push her to change her mind, and then she'd say I was being a spoiled brat and that I should think of the starving children who live on the streets and how could I be so selfish? And then I'd feel all humiliated and guilty and be sorry I'd asked for more."

Lost in her memories, Lisa took a deep breath and blew it out slowly. "I remember one day in particular, I must have been about nine. I was in the store watching my sister try on all her new clothes and I remember thinking that for the rest of my life I would always have to..."

Lisa started giggling. Her giggles grew bigger until finally she was laughing so hard she couldn't get her words out.

"What?" David asked.

But Lisa just kept on laughing.

"WHAAAT?" he yelled.

She put her hand to her mouth and tried to contain herself, but she just couldn't. She just laughed and laughed until finally David started laughing too. He couldn't help it. He had no idea what they were laughing about, but her laughter was so contagious that he simply couldn't help himself.

"I..." she began.

"I can't..."

David urged her on between his own snorts of laughter.

"I can't find a great guy because I have to settle for what I got!" She blurted out. She sat quietly for a moment and then her giggling started all over again. Her giggles grew to laughter and finally erupted into actual guffaws.

When she finally came up for air, Lisa wiped the laughter from her eyes, took a deep breath and continued. "I can't be in the world of dancing because I busted my leg and now I have to settle for what I got and I certainly can't have the body I want because I have to settle for what I..." and she started laughing so hard she doubled over and dropped her head on the table.

David instantly stopped laughing. He touched her arm and said "Lisa, is that true?"

"Is what true?" she asked, lifting her head slightly to see him.

"That you can't have the body you want or the man you want or the life of your dreams because you have to settle for what you got?" he said gently.

She looked at him from behind her fallen hair. New tears started in her eyes and her face took on an appearance that was unlike any David had ever seen. He instinctively knew that something important was happening.

"I don't have to settle for what I got?" she asked.

"That's not up to me, Lisa. It's *your* GUIDING RULE, not mine." David said wisely.

Lisa sat up and grabbed her paper napkin, making tightly screwed edges and then tearing them away. She sat intent on the napkin for a few minutes and then suddenly she dropped the napkin on the table and picked up her water.

"David, I'd like to propose a toast."

David picked up his glass. "Ok—go for it."

"To good friends who will tell you what you need to hear."

"To good friends!" David said as he clinked her glass with his.

They each took a sip and put down their glasses. The server passed by and Lisa waived her over.

"Can I get you something else?" she asked.

"Yes, please." Lisa took a big breath and went on. "This isn't what I ordered. I asked for a burger, medium, with mushrooms."

"What did you get instead?" the server asked.

"I'm not sure what it is," Lisa said cheerfully, "but I am sure of this: I'm not going to settle for something that I don't want!"

"Of course not, ma'am. I'll get your burger right out to you. Please accept my apology," the server said, as she picked up the plate and left their table.

"Oh wait a minute!" Lisa called after her.

"Yes?" the server said.

"Leave off the bun. And instead of onion rings, can I have a small salad with balsamic vinegar?" Lisa asked.

"How about a cookie? They just took some fresh ones out of the oven," the server tempted.

"No thanks," Lisa smiled. "I know exactly what I want and I won't settle for less!"

David looked at Lisa and took both her hands in his.

"Sounds like someone has a NEW GUIDING RULE" David said with a smile.

"Yep," Lisa said. *"I know exactly what I want and I won't settle for less!"*

She sat back in her chair with a peaceful calm and a palpable undercurrent of extreme excitement. It was like nothing David had ever experienced. It seemed at any minute she would burst from her seat as if propelled by a super jet engine.

He wondered if this was what Ted meant when he described the power band of the Action Formula and the synergy of the Internal Crew. Now more than ever, he wanted to go home and work his own formula.

"Hey you two look like you're having fun," Chelsea said as she walked up to the table. "What's new?"

"My rules," Lisa said triumphantly. She and David started laughing all over again as a totally confused Chelsea hung up her coat.

"So did you get the promotion?" David asked.

Chelsea sat back her chair and just stared at the menu.

- 12 -

Trust Your Instincts

David waited until Chelsea had ordered before he resumed the conversation. "So, what's new with you?" he asked.

"Actually, I've got some news," Chelsea said. "I..." She stopped mid-sentence as she looked at Lisa. Something was different about her, although Chelsea couldn't quite put her finger on what it was. "You look good, Lis. Did you get a haircut?"

"No, just a tune-up," Lisa smiled. "So what's your news?"

"I did it," Chelsea announced.

"You got the job?" David asked excitedly.

"Not exactly," Chelsea said mysteriously.

"Come on, Chels," Lisa urged, "Don't leave us dangling. What happened?"

"Well, I don't know if David told you, but we worked Ted's formula last week and David helped me figure out that my Action Formula was missing the RESOURCE component," Chelsea explained.

"Wow, David," Lisa smiled, "Haven't you been the helpful little motivation dude?" she added laughing.

"What do you mean?" Chelsea asked.

"David worked Ted's formula with me right before you got here. We found out I was stuck in the PERMISSION piece," Lisa announced proudly.

"Really! That's awesome! So did you figure it out?" Chelsea asked.

"Completely," Lisa reported proudly. "It's amazing how easy it was once I got going."

"VERY cool," Chelsea said, leaning over to give her a big hug. "So, what does that mean for you, then?"

"It means I'll be going in to see the principal tomorrow to talk about going part-time next year, and then I'll be calling a commercial realtor to start looking for space for my new dance studio. That is, right after I stop at the gym and buy a membership," Lisa said. "I've never felt like this, Chelsea. It's like my whole world has opened up to me."

"Oh Lisa, that's awesome! I'm so happy for you!" Chelsea exclaimed.

"So what's your news, Chelsea?" David interrupted. "I'm sorry, Lisa, but after everything we did on Chelsea's RESOURCE list, I'm dying to know what happened!"

"Well, I did exactly what we had planned, David. And I want to thank you again because going through those RESOURCE questions with you was a huge help to me." Chelsea said.

"Ok, sure, no problem. So what happened?!" David was starting to get agitated. "I can't stand the suspense!"

"Well, I did my presentation for Jeff and it went really well. In fact, he loved my plan for building up the region and was very impressed with my projections. He said it was *'creative and fresh'*—high praise coming from Jeff, believe me!" Chelsea added.

"And?" Lisa pressed.

"And he offered me the job with a huge salary increase and an embarrassingly high bonus and override," Chelsea announced.

"Chelsea, that's incredible! Congratulations!" Lisa jumped up to hug her.

Chelsea put out her hand to stop Lisa mid-step. "I turned it down."

"Of course you—wait! What?" Lisa stuttered.

"Chelsea, why?" David asked incredulously.

"Well, it was kind of weird," Chelsea began as Lisa stumbled back to her chair. "Right before I went in for my presentation, I started thinking about what Ted said about the Internal Crew"

"Yes," interjected Lisa, "That was so cool!"

"Right. So it struck me that I could consciously use my Internal Crew to actually solicit the kind of responses I wanted from Jeff's Internal Crew," Chelsea explained.

"Ok, I'm confused," Lisa said.

"No, I think I get it," David replied. "I did something like that with a member of my staff last week."

"Lisa, it was amazing. I used my Critic to engage Jeff and get him all riled up about how things had to change in the Region or we were going to lose major market share. It was much more powerful than the boring Analyst presentation that I had planned.

"Then I turned my Cheerleader loose to encourage him to think out of the box. I gave him a few compliments about the successful changes and bold moves he'd made in the past.

"Then I called up my Analyst to show him my plan and projections.

"And then I brought out my Force and got so passionate that Jeff got caught in my slipstream and actually applauded!" Chelsea was speaking so quickly, she had to stop to catch her breath. "Then, to top it all off, I asked him Ted's DESIRE questions. That caused Jeff to think about what was in it for him if he accepted my proposal. You should have seen him! He looked like a five year old kid at the circus, he was so giddy. I'm telling you it was the most exciting fifteen minutes of my entire career! And then..."

"Chelsea that's fantastic," David interrupted. "But I don't see where the *'I turned the job down'* part comes in."

"Oh, right. Sorry, I got carried away there," Chelsea laughed. "So, there I am doing the sales presentation of a lifetime—I did mention that right?"

"Yes, sweetie. Twice now," Lisa smiled.

"Right. So I'm looking at Jeff applauding—and this guy never applauds—and my Analyst suddenly whispered in my ear, *"Chels, if you can excite him that way, imagine what you could do selling something you actually believed in?"'*

David's mouth dropped open and Lisa leaned forward.

"And? And? And?" Lisa was bouncing in her chair.

"I turned it down." Chelsea paused slightly for dramatic effect, "And then I went back to my desk, cleared it out and put in my application for VP of Development at ACCDA."

"YES!" Lisa screamed. "This is the best news ever!"

"That's fantastic, Chelsea," David chimed in, *"You're perfect* for that job."

"Thanks, guys," Chelsea said humbly. "It just feels right, ya know?"

"Yes, I do know," Lisa said. "I know exactly what you mean. It's what happens when all your Internal Crew align to help you work The Action Formula—it's not like any feeling I've ever felt."

"It's kind of like Ted said," Chelsea added. "It's that powerband thing. Everything working together at optimal power and energy and you just speed into it like nobody's business. I just suddenly realized that I *could* be a good leader but that doing it for a cause I believe in would make my life complete."

Ever practical, David asked, "What about the money? I thought your BURNING DESIRE was to be able to make lots of money and show your daughters that you can be a mom *and* a successful businesswoman. Did I get that wrong?"

"No, that's right, David, and I haven't changed it. I just realized that I had it backwards. I had 'success' all wrapped up in *money* because that's what my Actor's rules were all about. I learned that from my dad. But when I thought about it, I realized that 'success' means something different for me than it did for my dad. To me, it's about making a difference.

"I love sales and marketing, but I want to make a greater impact than I can make with Jeff. He actually understood and congratulated me for my decision. He also asked me if I'd come back as a consultant and train the team to sell the way I'd just sold him. It was pretty amazing hearing him say that, I can tell you."

"Chelsea, you've got to be feeling pretty good right about now," Lisa said.

Chelsea folded her hands together on the table. "Yeah, I am. I mean, I know it's going to be a little harder financially for us, but the simple truth is that my Force is passionate about making a difference. And if I give up that part of my dream just to have a bigger house, then what am I really teaching my girls?" Her eyes were brimming with tears and yet she looked strong and in charge.

"You're going to rock that place," Lisa said, wiping her own tears with her napkin.

"I couldn't be more proud to be your friend, Chelsea," David added.

Chelsea looked at Lisa and David and felt the peace that comes when you're solid in your plan and safe in the support of your friends. For the first time in her life, she knew that she could handle anything. She was ready to kick it into high gear.

- 13 -

Find Your Inspiration

The roads had been plowed and it was eerily silent as David pulled out of the Corner Café parking lot. The moon was full and its light bounced off the snow covered trees so brilliantly that it was as if a blue spotlight shone down on the world.

"I wish I could see the ending for my book as clearly as I can see these pot holes," David thought driving carefully along the road.

Gillian was still in Miami and the idea of going home to an empty house had no appeal for him, so he decided to just drive around for a while. He had no particular destination in mind. As he drove past the Corner Café for the third time, he shook his head and smiled ironically at the way his laps around the block seemed to parallel his life.

Suddenly he felt a jolt go through his body. *"Everyone is getting what they want except me! Why can't I finish this book? I've got my RESOURCES. . . I don't think I have any PERMISSION barriers about it...Maybe it's the DESIRE thing. Maybe I just plain don't want to write a book."*

He leaned over and turned on the radio, surfing through stations until he found his favorite talk show.

"I'm completely lost," the voice said, *"I took care of my mom for two years. I gave up my job, I stopped going out with my friends and I devoted everything to taking care of her. I don't have any regrets about it, but now that she's gone I'm all alone. What am I supposed to do now that I don't have to count out pills three times a day?"*

"Slow and easy does it," the host replied. *"You have your entire life ahead of you. There's no rush at all."*

David slammed on the brakes and the car began to fishtail. His heart started pounding as he steered into the spin and brought the car safely to a stop.

"That's it!" David exclaimed. "It's been right there in front of me the entire time..."

- 14 -

Accelerate
And Go!

David closed the door to his brand new, shiny car and stood back to look at it one more time. He just couldn't get enough of admiring the sleek lines. As he walked around to help Gillian out of the car, he thought back on the past few years and smiled. So much had changed.

He handed his keys to the valet and offered Gillian his arm. They walked side-by-side into the enormous convention center and the sight took his breath away. That first glimpse *always* had this impact on him, and as they walked through the corridors, he made a silent promise to himself that he would never take any of this for granted.

Dozens of ushers moved through the crowd, collecting empty glasses and discarded cocktail napkins and encouraging the crowd to move through the multiple entrances to find their seats. Music filled the enormous hall, and colored spotlights swung around the room kissing the heads of the 3,000 excited attendees.

At one end of the hall stood a platform, decorated by banners with sponsors' logos on either side. And at the very back of the stage, hanging against the backdrop of the black velvet curtain, the ACCDA logo shone with the words that made this event ticket worth its price in gold.

Changing Lives with Creativity, Compassion and Commitment

Chelsea stood backstage with her clipboard, checking and double-checking each item on her list.

"We're at standing room only, Chelsea," her near-frantic assistant said, "What do you want me to do?"

She turned confidently and smiled to smooth his ruffled

feathers. "Tell Simon to go ahead and turn on the flat screens in the lobby and break out some more wine and hors d'oeuvres. They'll be fine out there."

"Got it," he said turning away. He stopped for a moment and came back over to her. "You've done an amazing job. I hope you feel good about all of this."

"Thanks, Brad. It was very much a team effort," she said humbly. Then she caught herself and added enthusiastically, "But it *is* pretty awesome, huh?"

"Unbelievable!" he said coming to life and offering her his fist. She bumped it with her own and wondered if high fives were now passé.

"Are we all set?" Lisa asked, running up and giving her a big hug.

"I am," Chelsea confirmed. "What about you?"

"We're good to go!" Lisa reported. "The kids are all dressed and waiting stage right. They're SO excited!"

"I can't wait to see them!" Chelsea gushed. "And Lisa, you really look amazing. That dress is so hot on you. Is that a size eight you're wearing?"

"Six," she beamed.

"You go girl!" Chelsea said as Lisa raised her hand for a high-five.

"Aha!" Chelsea thought smiling.

The houselights dimmed and the crowd burst into spontaneous applause as the conductor raised his baton.

"I guess some rules never go out of style, huh?" Lisa kidded.

"Shh! It's starting!" Chelsea whispered.

The violinists lifted their bows and the horns rang out as 47 children of all shapes and sizes danced their way onto the stage.

They moved with the energy and abandon that are reserved for our young, and they filled the stage with excitement and joy. As they moved into formation, the littlest member of the troupe got turned around and bounded dangerously close to the edge of the stage. Without missing a beat, the tallest boy nimbly moved towards her and shepherded her back to safety while the rest of the kids continued the routine with rhythmic panache.

Chelsea leaned in to Lisa. "They're so cute!"

"Shh!" Lisa hissed back, her eyes fixed on her little stars.

The kids moved together in perfect synchrony and as they twirled around the stage, Chelsea put her arm around Lisa.

"You did it, honey," Chelsea whispered. "They're wonderful."

"Yep," Lisa nodded. "They sure are."

The children bowed to thunderous applause and then bounded off the stage as Lisa ran to congratulate them.

Chelsea put down her clipboard and walked out to the podium at stage left. She stood motionless until the spotlight came on.

"Good evening, Ladies and Gentlemen, and welcome to the *AACDA Shatter Your Speed Limits Fund Raising Event.* I'm Chelsea Browdy, Vice President of Development."

The audience responded with polite applause and Chelsea nodded her head in thanks.

"We are so excited to have all of you with us tonight. As many of you know, thanks to our amazing sponsors, we have held 25 *Shatter Your Speed Limits* events in seven countries over the past two years, thereby raising awareness and funds at rates that many said couldn't be done."

The audience resumed their applause with greater vigor.

"Equally important, we have helped tens of thousands of people find greater happiness and fulfillment by attending our events, and we are thrilled to be able to offer this experience to you tonight!"

The applause intensified as the audience sent out whoops and whistles. *"Now they're ready,"* Chelsea thought.

"Now it is my great privilege to introduce to you our keynote speaker for tonight: a man who has clocked countless hours helping ACCDA for well over a decade, and a man I'm proud to call my dear friend. But before I call him out here, I'd like to tell you a little story about your speaker that you may not know.

"I first met David a little over 15 years ago when I was volunteering at City Hospital. I was heading to the cafeteria one day when I literally bumped into him as he walked through the halls. He was completely disheveled and looked totally lost, so I asked him where he was headed. He just kept walking with his head down and mumbled something about going to the parking lot. So, I explained that he was taking the long way around the hospital and offered to show him a shortcut.

"Of course, I expected him to take me up on it but instead he just stopped walking and looked up at me with this eerie, blank expression. So, I repeated my offer and said, *'Sir, do you want me to show you the quickest way out?'* He just shrugged his shoulders and with complete despair he asked, 'What's The Rush?'

"Ladies and Gentlemen, please help me welcome the author of the New York Times Best Seller, *What's The Rush?* Please put your hands together for Mr. David Morris!"

Chelsea applauded enthusiastically as David strode onto the stage. To her delight, the audience rose to their feet with electric energy to welcome him. Giving David a quick hug, she gracefully stepped aside and gave him the stage. Once out of the spotlight, she trotted down the stage steps to take her seat in the front row. She sat between Gillian and Lisa and then quickly leaned over Lisa's lap to say hi to Lisa's fiancé, Nathan.

Chelsea's daughters were sitting in the second row behind her and Brooke leaned forward to whisper in her ear, "I'm really proud of you mom."

"Thanks, honey!" Chelsea whispered with tears in her eyes.

David bowed his head to the audience and then lifted his hands inviting them to take their seats. He left the podium and walked down to the lip of the stage to be closer to his audience. His 3,000 fans responded by leaning in.

"Ladies and Gentlemen, what do you do when everything you've always known suddenly isn't?" he began.

"My story is no different than many of yours. She gave birth to me, she took care of me and she taught me that the best ice cream is the kind you eat right from the container. She taught me about how to behave in public and what kind of flowers to buy for my date. She taught me what to do and she taught me what not to do. She tied my shoes and bandaged my wounds and she stayed up nights worrying about whether I'd be okay.

"And then, one day, the tides turned and suddenly it was I who took care of her and it was I who told her what to do and what not to do and it was I who tied her shoes and it was I who bandaged her wounds and it was I who stayed up nights worrying if she'd be okay.

"Just as she had done for me my entire life, I put myself aside and cared for her. It was my privilege and my honor to give back a tiny piece of the care she'd given me, and while it wasn't always easy, it was always the right thing to do. And when she was finally released from the prison that had become her life, I—like many of you—felt lost and alone.

"I knew I should give her clothes to the poor, but when I walked into her closet and smelled her perfume I thought, **what's the rush?**

"I knew I should ready her house for sale but it was the middle of winter so I figured, **what's the rush?**

"I knew I should resume my life and move back to the city, but there was nothing waiting for me there so I wondered, **what's the rush?**

"My friends invited me to their homes to meet single women who would bring me companionship but I declined their offers thinking, **what's the rush?**

"And then one day I decided to write a book so that I could help others as they too became their parents' parents. But week after week went by and the pages lay blank and I just figured. . ."

"What's the rush?" his fans called out.

"Chelsea recruited me to volunteer for ACCDA and I jumped in like the desperate man I was, starved for a project and unable to launch my own. I logged more hours in Board meetings than I can count while we batted around go-nowhere fundraising ideas that barely covered the coffee we served at our meetings. I kept thinking there was more we could be doing but after all..."

"What's the rush?" more people joined in.

"I remember sitting with my friends after a meeting in which we had asked our members to accelerate their thinking so we could expand our reach and raise awareness worldwide.

But for every great idea we offered, there were so many reasons not to change, so many rules to be followed, so much fear to be addressed and I just figured..."

"What's the rush?" the whole audience chanted in unison.

"And then one day I got an email from my friend, Ted. Ted had been a major contributor to our organization, as a volunteer, a Board member and a donor. He logged thousands of hours of service, constantly putting everyone's needs before his own.

"Ted told me about a formula that he'd learned that enabled him to change his life and get everything he had always wanted while at the same time making major strides for the company he worked for and a huge difference for the people of a developing country.

"Ladies and Gentlemen, Ted found something we all search for—a brand new roadmap that

- Illuminated the path to a safe and happy life for his family,
- Allowed him to experience every single day to the fullest,
- Enabled him to make a difference for thousands of people,
- Brought him tremendous joy and lots of cool toys, and
- Made it possible for him to establish a solid reputation for excellence in his industry.

"Perhaps the most amazing part of all of this was that he accomplished it all in less than a year."

The audience broke into applause.

"Once Ted was sure the formula worked, he had the grace to share it with me. I'm ashamed to admit that when he first told me about it, I thought it was just the mad ravings of a stressed out CFO. But when I saw what his formula did for my friends I realized I'd been very wrong.

"I derived great joy in watching them build the lives they'd always wanted and so I decided to try it with my team at work. I applied Ted's formula throughout my department and in record time we made exponential changes in our team's productivity and our revenues broke industry standards. Needless to say, my boss was thrilled. I emailed Ted about it and he wrote back something I'll never forget. He said, *'Success is greatest when everyone works The Action Formula together.'*

"Then one night I was driving in my car and I heard a radio announcer say something that stopped me dead in my tracks. He was interviewing someone who had lost her mom and she sounded just like I had felt so many years ago. The way he helped her was to tell her to slow down and not rush things. He told her she had plenty of time.

"Ladies and gentlemen, how many of you have missed opportunities in life while you waited for just the right moment?"

Hundreds of hands shot up in the audience.

"How many of you do what I used to do: postpone, procrastinate and put off things that you really want to do because you just can't get motivated to make it happen. Can any of you relate to that?"

More hands went up as people snickered and nodded knowingly to each other.

"Well that night a fire ignited in my gut, and for the first time I really understood what my friend Ted meant when he said that we all have to find our deepest DESIRES. Suddenly, I didn't want to waste one more moment of my life. I decided to change and vowed that I would no longer postpone my life. The first thing I did was pick up my cell phone and program my speed dial!"

The audience broke into laughter and applauded, as scattered people turned to their neighbors whispering comments like, *"I really need to do my taxes!"* and *"I still haven't programmed my DVR!"*

"Next, I sent an email out to the members of the Board of AACDA and suggested a retreat to talk about how we could use Ted's formula to increase our impact. I'm proud to report that since we held that meeting, we have doubled our volunteer base and dramatically expanded our reach worldwide—and this is in spite of a difficult economy!"

More cheers and applause.

"In the meantime, my friend Ted was happy in his new life and was doing such a strong service for his company, they allowed him to live there permanently. We talked via email at least once a week, and video-conferenced whenever time would allow. I continued to send him reports of the impact his formula was having on everyone here and that meant more to him than I can express.

"Ted had been down there for about two years when I got an email that was addressed from him but the subject line was left blank. I found that kind of odd because, as many of you know, Ted never left out any details."

A few audience members laughed appreciatively.

"Ladies and Gentlemen, I'd like to read that email to you now:

FROM: Ted@TheActionFormula.com
TO: David
SUBJECT:

Dear David,

It is with deep sadness that I'm writing to tell you that Ted died last week. He was where he most wanted to be, on his beloved boat with the boys by his side.

Ted had evidently been ill for quite some time, though he kept it from us until the very end. I guess we'll never know whether this was in some way related to the stress of our past. What we do know is that he died as he had lived, thinking only of how he could make our lives better.

I thought you'd want to know that you were very much on his mind in the last days of his life. He wrote a last email to you, but the storm came in before he could get it off to you and by the time we were back on line, it was too late. I'm forwarding that email to you now.

Thank you for being such a good friend to my husband. You meant the world to him.

Ruth.

David looked up from the page. "Underneath Ruth's email there was a short email from Ted—Here are my friend's last words to me:

FROM: Ted@TheActionFormula.com
TO: David
SUBJECT: Important

David -

I don't have a lot of time because there's a big storm brewing here, but I want to send you a quick email because there's something important I need to tell you.

I must confess to you, my friend, that I'm worried about you. You remind me of the me of yesterday. You work too hard, David. You take care of everyone else and you never think about yourself and what would make your heart sing. That's not valiant, David. That's just stupid.

So listen to me now. I wasted far too many years pushing aside what I truly wanted for the sake of living up to rules that I had adopted before I knew any better. The end result was that I lost out on the richness of what life has to offer. Thank God I discovered the formula to get out of that hole or I might never have known the bliss of the past two years with Ruth and the boys. But I'm filled with

---

regret for the time we lost together while I was stuck in my rules.

I want you to know that I finally discovered the answer to the question you've been asking ever since the day your mother died. I know how it has plagued you.

The answer is: big.

There's a really BIG rush, David.

Don't waste another minute to go after what you really want. Step on the gas pedal my friend. Use the Action Formula. Shatter your speed limits and get everything you truly want. Do it now before you miss your chance.

T.

David looked up from Ted's letter. The stage lights were hot white and blurred through his dampened eyes. He couldn't see the woman in the second row reach over to take her husband's hand. Nor could he see the man in the seventh row pull his child onto his lap. Like Ted, David would never fully know the impact he'd made.

"Ladies and Gentlemen," David continued, "You came here tonight to learn how to shatter your speed limits and we have great speakers lined up for you to help you do just that. Open your hearts and your minds. Work Ted's formula so you can find your deepest DESIRE, gather your RESOURCES and give yourself PERMISSION to get what you truly want for yourself, your family, your friends and your business. And then use the formula to make an impact on every life you touch.

"But please, remember my friend Ted's last words: There is a rush. There's a really *big* rush. Speed counts.

"So make tonight count. Make tonight the night you say 'no' to failure and 'yes' to success.

"Make tonight the night you shatter your speed limits so you can get what you truly want all the time in record time.

"Are you ready to start your engines? Say, 'Yes!'"

Three thousand voices simultaneously screamed out "YES!" as the crowd jumped to their feet in thunderous applause. The orchestra joined in, sending out a brilliant overture to their future.

David bowed deeply and then stood erect, extending his hands outward to acknowledge the audience. He walked to the side of the stage and clapped in the direction of Chelsea and Lisa and threw a tender kiss to Gillian.

Finally, David turned his head upward, closed his eyes and whispered the two words that had become his mantra,

"Thanks, Ted."

FAST TRACK

How long are you willing to wait to get what you truly want?

Life is short. Start now!

Author's Note

I'd like to take a quick moment to thank you for reading this book. I truly hope you found solutions that will help you build and grow your business and thrive in every area of your life. I also hope that once you've mastered the Action Formula and used it to shatter your speed limits, you'll in turn help others by sharing it with them. Be a Ted to the people in your life—at work, at home and everywhere in between.

Now that you've finished the book, I think it's time that we work together to bust a major myth:

Motivation gurus have often told us, *"It's not the destination—it's the journey."* What they meant is that the most important things in life shouldn't be the destination (what we want) but rather the journey (the road we took to get what we want).

Gurus tell us this for one reason: because at the end of their lives too many people are filled with regret for having missed the joy of their daily lives while chasing after their dreams. So what the gurus *mean* is that we shouldn't lose perspective and make the destination all that matters. That makes sense.

But exactly how much less emphasis should we put on the destination? Ten percent? Twenty percent? Thirty? Forgive me gurus, but perhaps we need to change the rule on this one. I think the answer is to decide what we truly want, gather our resources, lock in our permissions and go for it. When we use the Action Formula to guide us we can totally enjoy the journey—particularly since we get to the destination so much faster.

So let's not downplay the destination. Let's *UP*-play the destination and then help everyone get there faster!

New Rule: It's Not the Journey—it's the Destination.

I'm not saying that the journey can't be fun or enriching in and of itself. However if you're headed for some place really special, would you rather take three connecting flights or figure out how to fly directly so you can spend more time enjoying your destination and sharing it with those you love? That's entirely your decision to make. My clients choose the fast track. For that matter, so do I.

If you're not living the life that you really want, if your family isn't as happy as they could be, if your organization isn't living up to its full potential or if you don't wake up every single morning delighted with the person who greets you in the mirror, then please, do something about it. Quit trying to trick yourself into believing that you don't *really* want the things you dream of. Embrace the life you have because it is the springboard for whatever comes next, but for goodness sake, don't give up on what you truly want. Just follow this roadmap and get there faster:

DESIRES + RESOURCES + PERMISSION = ACTION!

If you hit a pot hole, come up to a barrier or get lost along the way, please know that you don't have to ride this road alone! Just go to my blog at www.ShatterYourSpeedLimits. com and I will be there for you. Ask me your questions and I will answer you personally.

But please—start right away. The simple and sad reality is that life is far too short. Don't waste one more precious moment of it. *Start now.*

Shatter your speed limits and I'll look forward to seeing you on the fast track!

Wendy

158

Acknowledgements

There's a very good reason that so many authors include an acknowledgement section in their books. The simple truth is that no one achieves success alone. As those who have come before me, I feel compelled to share with you the names of some of the people who influenced me before and during the creation of this book. I can't possibly list everyone, but I'd like to tell you about some extra special people who have helped or inspired me to shatter my own speed limits.

First and foremost, I'd like to thank all of the men and women who bravely allowed me to experiment as I developed the Action Formula and discovered all of its many applications in organizational and personal development. Their very real triumphs, challenges and tragedies served as the foundation for this story and brought life to the characters of Ted, David, Chelsea and Lisa.

I'd also like to acknowledge the millions of men and women worldwide who work so passionately to make a difference for people most of us will never meet. I'm proud to say that this book is the first of its type to spotlight non-profit organizations and I hope it will send a strong message of thanks for the untiring work that is being done to help wherever help is needed. More than that, I hope it will help to raise significant funds and awareness for important causes, since I will be using the book (along with associated events) to benefit charities around the globe. Just for the record, "AACDA" is a fictional organization created solely for the purposes of this story but it represents many of the non-profit groups I've worked with through the years.

My book marketing guru Steve Harrison influenced me more than I can express. Steve has an uncanny and unique talent that enables him to identify and express the needs of a target audience, and he helps authors get their messages heard by learning to do the same. The best way I can describe his talent is to tell you that it was he who helped me create the title of this book during an invigorating brainstorming session that was the epitome of what creative teamwork is supposed to be. He has taught me more about the world of publishing and media than I ever knew existed and has introduced me to some amazing people including his brother and brilliant partner, Bill Harrison, the talented Geoffrey Berwind and the exceptional Nancy Ipolitti. Steve has honored me with his friendship and continues to inspire me with his drive to make sure that no one goes to their grave with their song still in them.

My editor extraordinaire, Tim Boden did more than help me dot my i's and cross my t's. Tim answered my prayer for a skilled set of eyes that would challenge my thinking, expand my perspective and correct my errors. The icing on the cake was the bonus of sensitivity and compassion that he brought to the story. He treated my characters as family and my words as precious stones that needed polishing and helped me to shape this book with the precision touch of a master.

My layout designer, webmaster and friend, Chase Rogers, allowed me to turn my dreams into reality with his unwavering patience, incredible talent and extraordinary skills. Chase consistently shatters the limits of technology to make room for creativity and originality and continually delights me with new possibilities in visual art and efficiency on all of my websites.

One of the most difficult steps of book publishing is creating a cover that effectively portrays the heart and soul of the author's message. George Foster came through for me in living color with his unique and powerful design that completely captured every metaphor and nuance of this story. Simply brilliant.

My pre-publication reviewers did me a tremendous honor by previewing the manuscript and providing their endorsements (their complete and unedited reviews are printed at the beginning of this book). It isn't easy being asked to review someone's work and I'm truly grateful to all of you for taking the time to make sure this message would be helpful to others. I must say, there is nothing in life that quite equals the heart-pounding moment when we open the email of someone we hold on a pedestal, clutching the mouse and praying that the response will say anything other than "it sucked." Thank you for choosing other words.

Next, I'd like to acknowledge some of the heroes who have inspired me by the ways in which they have shattered their speed limits.

Barbra Streisand (my first and greatest inspiration-if you only knew the impact you've had on my life), Celine Dion, Carole King, Bette Midler, Edith Piaf, Sir Paul McCartney, Sir Elton John, James Taylor and countless other artists who didn't allow anyone to talk them out of pursuing their dreams to live in the music.

Oprah Winfrey, Barbara Walters, Katie Couric, Diane Sawyer, Whoopi Goldberg and Ellen Degeneris for bravely allowing their vulnerability and authenticity to shine through the camera lens week after week. You set the bar higher and higher yet always made that bar seem attainable.

Emmit Smith, Troy Aikman, Brett Favre, Joe Montana, Peyton Manning, Danica Patrick, Richard Petty, Roger Bannister, Usain Bolt, Michael Phelps, Tiger Woods and all of the athletes who shatter speed limits season after season. I'm in awe of how you make your bodies do things I can't even imagine imagining.

Steve Jobs, Bill Gates, Mark Zuckerberg, Donald Trump, Mary Kay Ash, Debbie Fields, Estee Lauder, Jack Welch, Anita Roddick, Madame C.J. Walker, Lee Iacocca, Warren Buffet, Jerry Jones, Nancy Collins and all of the entrepreneurial geniuses who have proven that there is no ceiling on success.

Earl Nightingale, Dale Carnegie, Fred Pryor, Stephen Covey, Jack Canfield, Mark Victor Hansen, Brian Tracy, Tom Hopkins, Zig Ziglar, Chip and Dan Heath, Dr. Spencer Johnson, Ken Blanchard, Tom Peters, Brendon Burchard, Denis Waitley and all of the gurus who gave us practical tools that we could use to enhance our lives.

The doctors and their staff whose lives most will never understand. You shatter speed limits every day fighting an ugly war to help us live our lives just a little longer or at the very least to live and die with some semblance of dignity.

Our military men and women. There aren't enough words for the risks you take and the limits you shatter every single day. Thank you.

This list is by no means exhaustive.

Check **www.ShatterYourSpeedLimits.com/heros** for ongoing updates as I continue to discover people who are shattering their speed limits. And be sure to let me know of anyone you think I should know about!

SHATTER YOUR SPEED LIMITS RESOURCES

Shatter Your Speed Limits Online

"Success is greatest when everyone works The Action Formula together." –Ted

Visit us at ShatterYourSpeedLimits.com and discover lots of FREE RESOURCES to help you to accelerate your journey and reach your destination.

Follow Wendy's blog and get ongoing training to help you Shatter Your Speed Limits—absolutely FREE.

Download FREE articles and videos and learn how to:
> ➤ Exponentially increase your sales (whatever the venue)
> ➤ Take your relationships to a significantly higher level
> ➤ Master the art of platform speaking
> ➤ Sell more when you speak
> ➤ Write and publish your own book
> ➤ Get free publicity
> ➤ Organize your house and get rid of clutter
> ➤ Lose weight and keep it off
> ➤ Brand and market your expertise
> ➤ Get and stay fit
> ➤ Find your soul mate and live happily ever after
> ➤ Retire early and live in style
> ➤ Maximize your social networking power
> ➤ Conquer the job market

➤ Accelerate your online business
➤ Get known as an expert in your field
➤ Create a self-driven team
➤ Create healthy meals in record time
➤ Move from weekend athlete to pro
➤ Resolve conflicts at work and home
  And lots more!

We're constantly updating our FREE RESOURCES knowledge base, so stop by the website often and grab everything you need to Shatter Your Speed Limits!

While you're on the website, be sure to let us know of your successes. Your journey will inspire others to use the formula and shatter their speed limits so pass it forward! And if you have any questions along the way—just ask Wendy and she'll answer you personally. Wendy is connected to lots of brilliant experts and between all of them you will get the RESOURCES you need to get where you want to go!

Visit Us Soon At

www.ShatterYourSpeedLimits.com

Shatter Your Speed Limits Live Events

Want to seriously fast-track your success? Attend one of our **Shatter Your Speed Limits Live Events** and work with Wendy for an afternoon or an entire weekend!

Wendy and her team will take you through the Action Formula one step at a time and get you on the fast track to success! In a high energy, interactive program, you'll:

➤ Discover and crystallize your most burning DESIRES
➤ Identify all of the RESOURCES you need to be able to get what you want
➤ Break your old rules and lock in your PERMISSION to accelerate and capture everything you truly want

This event will change your life forever and propel you to your destination faster than you ever dreamed possible!

Register online at **www.ShatterYourSpeedLimits. com** for priority notification of Shatter Your Speed Limits events being held near you and you could win a ticket for you and your guest to attend our next live event absolutely free!

Shatter Your Speed Limits Personal Coaching

How much faster could you get what you truly want if you had a "Ted" in your life—your own personal coach and mentor—someone who would walk you through the Action Formula and help you get to where you want to go faster and easier?

How much further and faster could you go if you had an expert you could call–email–or chat with whenever you need help?

We will be your Ted.

Our **Shatter Your Speed Limits Personal Coaching Program** is customized to your specific DESIRES to help you gather your RESOURCES and lock in your PERMISSIONS. You'll get private coaching by one of our amazing Fast-Track Coaches at a pace that fits your style and needs.

The journey is richer and faster when you've got a "Ted" in your life.

For more information,

Visit Us Soon At
www.ShatterYourSpeedLimits.com

Shatter Your Speed Limits Organizational Training Programs

Want to fast-track the success of your organization? Our **Shatter Your Speed Limit Training Programs** are specifically designed to enable you to achieve your goals in record time.

Our team of experts will help you to shatter your organizational speed limits with fast-paced, entertaining seminars and workshops providing you and your team with proven strategies to:

➤ Exponentially increase sales revenues,

➤ Measurably improve productivity,

➤ Significantly streamline communications,

➤ Dramatically enhance teamwork and collegiality

And more.

Visit our website at **www.ShatterYourSpeedLimits.com** to learn more about how we can help you and your team shatter your speed limits this year*!

*Mention Ted's name in our first conversation and get 10% off of your first training program!

ATTENTION: Non-Profit Organizations

The Shatter Your Speed Limits Team is committed to making a significant difference worldwide. If you are involved in serving a non-profit organization, contact us soon to discuss how we can partner together to raise funds and awareness for your organization.

Nothing would give us more pleasure than to help you and your team Shatter Your Speed Limits this year and increase your impact with those you serve!

Visit **www.ShatterYourSpeedLimits.com/non-profits** to learn about how we may be able to help you raise more funds and awareness.

Book Wendy To Speak at Your Next Event

Wendy Lipton-Dibner has been helping people shatter their speed limits for over 25 years. Known internationally for her high-energy programs, meeting planners know they can count on Wendy to provide keynotes that are as entertaining and inspiring as they are practical and informative.

Wendy's eclectic background allows her to bring a unique perspective to the platform. Her materials include step-by-step proven formulas tested over the course of her career in the social sciences, healthcare, organizational and personal development, and in retail and corporate sales and leadership.

One-part entertainer, one-part trainer and one-part motivator, Wendy uses her unusual combination of quick intellect, deep compassion and sharp wit to create what she calls "an emotional roller coaster ride" for her audiences. She inspires everyone to make clear distinctions between opinions, facts and feelings and entices them to make immediate and permanent changes—personally and professionally.

When Wendy speaks, people change. They change how they think, they change how they feel, they change what they do and they change what they get. Her results are even stronger than her presentations.

Contact Wendy to discuss how she can help your audience shatter their speed limits!

Visit Us Soon At
www.ShatterYourSpeedLimits.com

About The Author

Wendy Lipton-Dibner M.A. is known internationally for her uncanny ability to move people to action. President and Founder of Professional Impact, Inc., she works passionately as a speaker, author and consultant, helping her clients avoid the frustration of failure and the tragedy of a life half-lived. An expert in organizational and personal development, Wendy wakes up every day excited about knowing precisely what she wants and how to make it happen. But she didn't start that way.

Some kids know exactly who they are and what they want to be when they grow up. They are comfortable in their own skin, they set their course and they never look back. But Wendy wasn't like that. In fact, she spent her first 30 years searching for the unique impact she could make in the world. Wendy reinvented herself over and over, adding layers of education, certification and skills until she had amassed a wealth of knowledge and experiences. All the while she was desperately searching for the answers to the questions: Who am I and what do I really want?

Her existential quest sent her on quite a journey: Her passion for music led her to perform in vocal groups and theater productions. Her love of teaching prompted her to serve as a university instructor. Her talent for research brought her to work as a project manager in organizational research—publishing her results in professional journals and presenting them at the U.S. Senate. Her entrepreneurial drive compelled her to build a full-service spa where she broke industry standards for retail sales. Her deep desire to make a difference drove her to receive certification as a psychotherapist and open a private practice, and then to purchase a motivation franchise where she set world records for sales and customer service.

But something was still missing and Wendy was desperate to find it.

She cleared her calendar and left for a 7-day cruise. Alone in the middle of the ocean, she made a list of everything she'd ever done, everything she knew how to do, everything she loved doing, everything she dreamed of doing and all of the rules that were getting in her way. One by one, she rejected the rules that were holding her back and then stared at her list of desires and resources, hoping they would reveal some new truth.

Then on the last day of the cruise, she found it—the career that would allow her to do everything she loved while making a significant impact: She would combine her unique set of knowledge, skills and insights into practical and inspiring programs and then deliver them on stages worldwide. The moment she returned, she sprang to action with an energy and passion that was greater than any she had ever known. Within three months she launched her new career as a professional speaker with a mission to make an impact on every life she touched. And she has.

Everywhere she speaks, Wendy uses the Action Formula as the foundation for her programs, assuring that her audiences make catalytic changes in record time. Her high-energy, entertaining style, coupled with her practical strategies for motivation, alignment and differentiation have enabled healthcare organizations, small businesses and Fortune 500 companies to increase productivity and revenues exponentially. A stickler for measured results, Wendy's research has consistently revealed that productivity and excellence are directly correlated with the degree to which people are internally motivated, able to do the job and willing to change. Her commitment to addressing all three components of success has helped tens of thousands of people worldwide improve their satisfaction and results in business and in life.

With the publication of Shatter Your Speed Limits™, she is shaking things up yet again—sharing her motivation secrets and making a public commitment to use her expertise as a vehicle to help non-profit organizations raise funds and increase public awareness. Never one to be stuck in status quo, Wendy walks her talk by continually asking herself the question that is at the very core of The Action Formula:

If you woke up tomorrow morning and magically found that you had everything you truly wanted—how would your life be different?

Today Wendy teaches what she wishes she'd known long ago— that existential crises are the springboards for reinvention and that wondering who you are and what you truly want is always the perfect place to begin.

Visit Us Soon At
www.ShatterYourSpeedLimits.com

173

Made in the USA
Charleston, SC
19 June 2011